CONSTANZE DIEHL-HUPFER • MAGDALENA MELZER

AF598777

CROCHET IN BLACK & WHITE

BOLD TWO-COLOR DESIGNS FOR YOU AND YOUR HOME

Trafalgar Square
North Pomfret, Vermont

First published in the United States of America
in 2016 by
Trafalgar Square Books
North Pomfret, Vermont 05053

Originally published in German as *Black & White*.

Copyright © 2015 Constanze Diehl-Hupfer, Magdalena Melzer, and frechverlag GmbH
English translation © 2016 Trafalgar Square Books

This edition is published by arrangement with Claudia Böhme Rights & Literacy Agency, Hannover, Germany (www.agency-boehme.com).

All rights reserved. No part of this book may be reproduced, by any means, without written permission of the publisher, except by a reviewer quoting brief excerpts for a review in a magazine, newspaper or web site.

The instructions and material lists in this book were carefully reviewed by the author and editor; however, accuracy cannot be guaranteed. The author and publisher cannot be held liable for errors.

ISBN: 978-1-57076-788-3

Library of Congress Control Number: 2016948647

PRODUCT MANAGEMENT: Judith Wiedemann
EDITING: no:vum, Susanne Noll, Hennef
PHOTOS: frechverlag GmbH, 70499 Stuttgart; lichtpunkt, Michael Ruder, Stuttgart
HAIR AND MAKEUP: Diekmann Face Art, Ludwigsburg
MODELS: Constanze Diehl-Hupfer (pages 6-11, 26-28, 32/33, 54-56, 60-63, 76-81, 84-93); Magdalena Melzer (pages 12-25, 29-31, 34-39, 42-53, 57-59, 64/65, 68-75, 82/83)
LAYOUT: Petra Theilfarth
TRANSLATION: Donna Druchunas

Printed in China

10 9 8 7 6 5 4 3 2 1

CONTENTS

HOME SWEET HOME

JUST FOR FUN

HOME WORK

Introduction

No matter where you look these days, you can't miss the trend of black and white design. It's everywhere: in the world of fashion, in lifestyle magazines, and on style blogs. It was only a matter of time before black-and-white fever hit the DIY and handmade scene!

The look is modern and simple. Black and white accessories are basics that go with any style. Living rooms can be spruced up using black-and-white décor, with color accents added to make a special piece shine. The photos in this book will provide inspiration and ideas for what you can do in your own space.

Bold designs and clean lines make it all possible. You can even crochet art to hang on the wall! And graphic table runners and cushions will draw you in. Why wait? Get started today and introduce the black-and-white trend into your house from room to room.

In these pages, you'll find patterns for crocheted accessories as well as plenty of items to decorate your home and make it more functional. This trend is just waiting for you to pick up your hook. Have fun with our black-and-white crochet!

Constanze Diehl-Hupfer Magdalena Melzer

HOME
SWEET
HOME

MUSIC IS MY FIRST LOVE

A PAIR OF PILLOWS

SKILL LEVEL

Intermediate

PILLOW WITH APPLIQUÉ NOTES

FINISHED MEASUREMENTS:

Approx. 16 x 16 in / 40 x 40 cm

MATERIALS

Yarn: CYCA #5 (chunky/craft/rug) Schachenmayr Bravo Mezzo or equivalent (100% acrylic; 180 yd/165 m / 100 g), White #01, 300 g

CYCA #3 (DK/light worsted) Schachenmayr Bravo or equivalent (100% acrylic; 146 yd/133 m / 50 g), Black #8226, 50 g

Hooks: U.S. size E-4 / 3.5 mm and U.S. size 7 / 4.5 mm

Notions: 3 buttons, approx. ¾ in / 2 cm in diameter, 16 x 16 in / 40 x 40 cm pillow form, tapestry needle, sewing needle and matching thread

Gauge: 10 sts and 10 rows = 4 x 4 in / 10 x 10 cm in Main Pattern with larger hook. Adjust needle size to obtain correct gauge if necessary.

Chart: Page 94

PILLOW WITH LARGE NOTE

FINISHED MEASUREMENTS:

Approx. 20 x 20 in / 50 x 50 cm

MATERIALS

Yarn: CYCA #5 (chunky/craft/rug) Schachenmayr Bravo Mezzo or equivalent (100% acrylic; 180 yd/165 m / 100 g)

Yarn Amounts:
White #01, 300 g
Black #99, 100 g

Hook: U.S. size H-8 / 5 mm

Notions: Tapestry needle, 4 buttons, approx. ¾ in / 2 cm in diameter, 20 x 20 in / 50 x 50 cm pillow form, sewing needle and matching thread

Gauge: 10 hdc and 10 rows = 4 x 4 in / 10 x 10 cm. Adjust needle size to obtain correct gauge if necessary.

Chart: Page 100

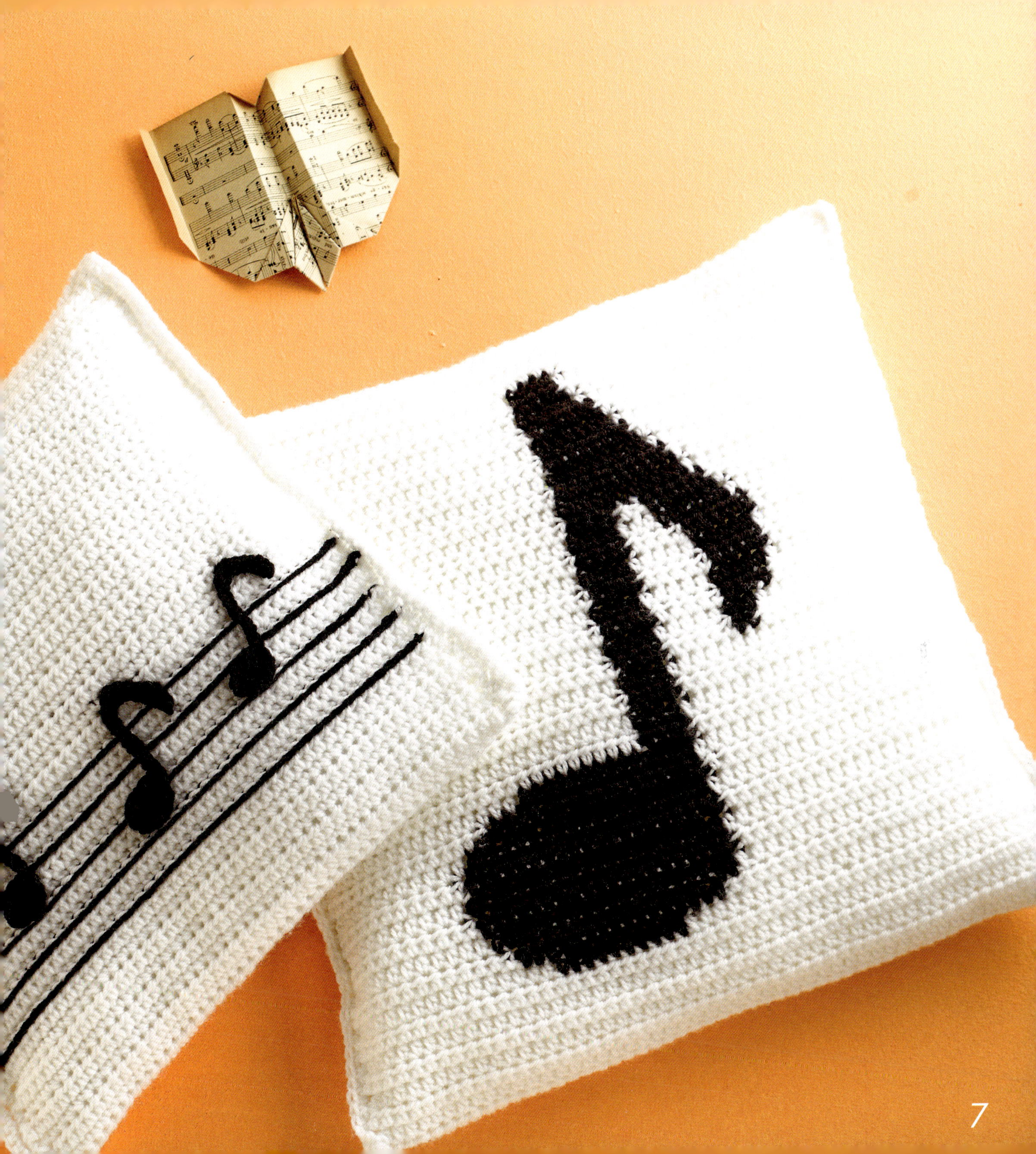

in / 30 cm down. The top should overlap the bottom by 3 in / 8 cm and the pillow should measure 17¼ in / 44 cm. Join the side edges

INSTRUCTIONS

Turning chains: Begin each row of sc with ch 1. Begin each row of hdc with ch 2.

With White and larger hook, ch 47.
Row 1 (RS): Sc in 2nd ch from hk and in each ch across (46 sts).
Row 2 (WS): Hdc in each sc across (46 sts).
Rows 3–26: Work in Main Pattern.
Row 27: Working into back loops only, sc in each sc across (46 sts).
Row 28: Hdc in each sc across (46 sts).
Rows 29–36: Rep Rows 28 and 28.
Rows 37–91: Work in Main Pattern.
Piece should measure 34½ in / 88 cm.
Rows 92 and 93: Work Buttonhole Band.

MUSIC NOTES

Make 3.
With Black and smaller hook, make a magic ring and work music note as charted.

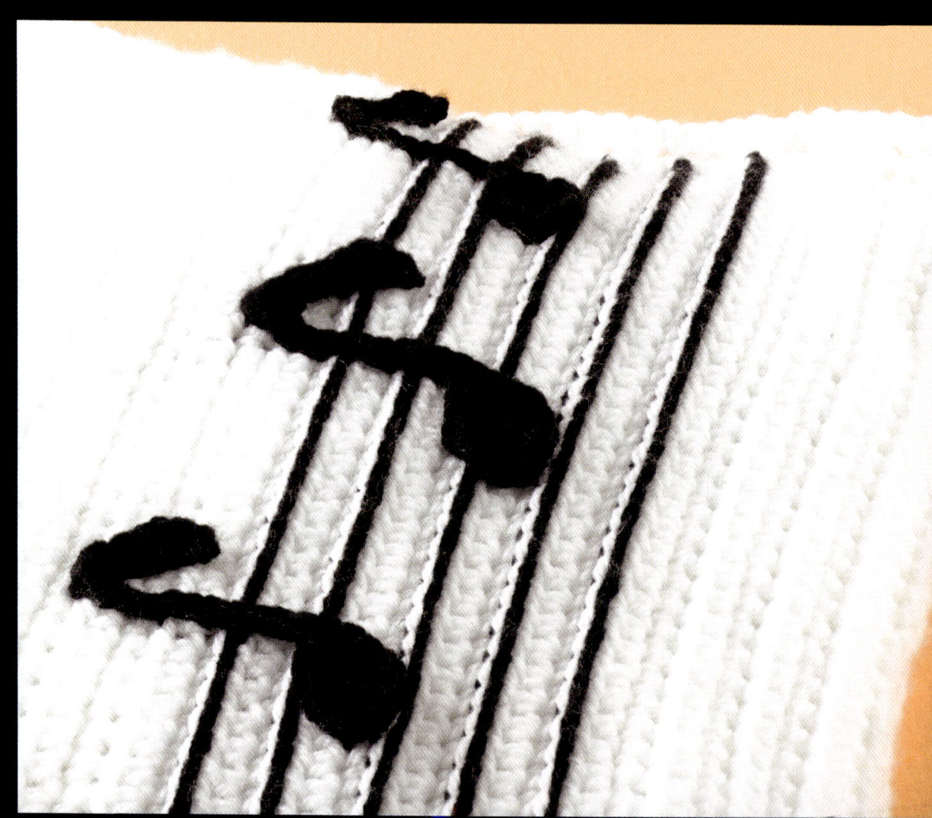

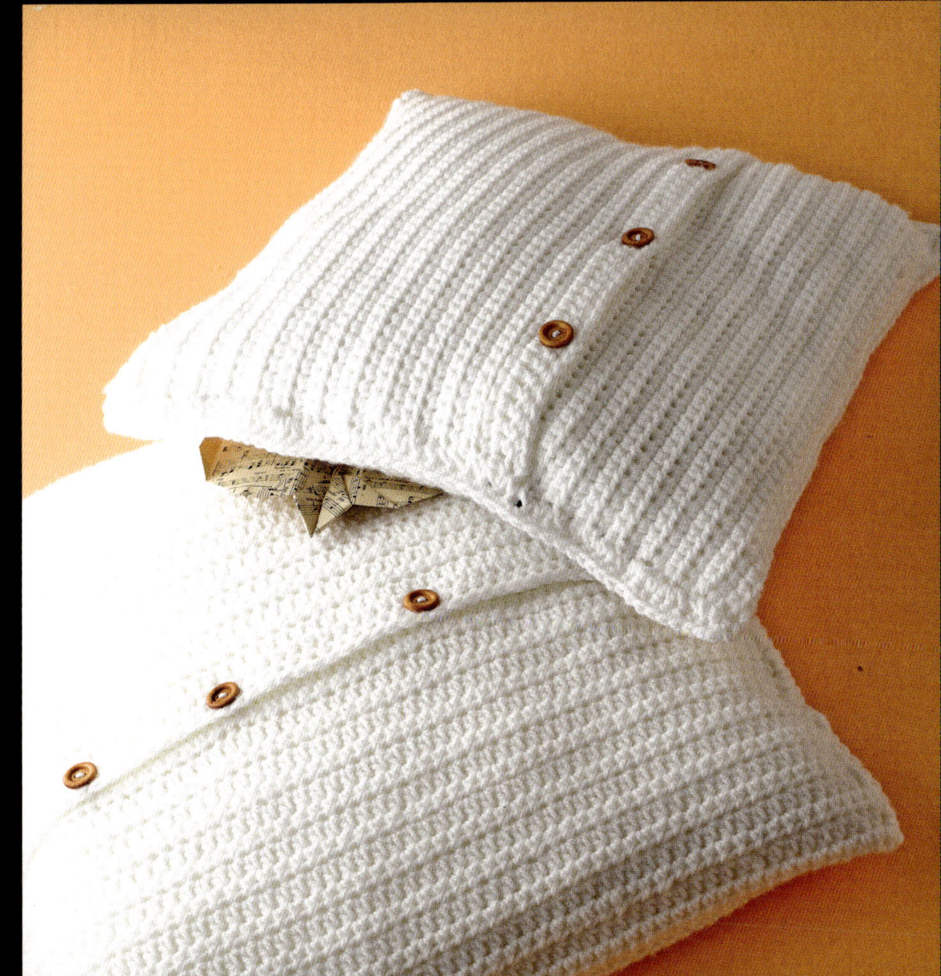

PILLOW WITH LARGE NOTE

BUTTONHOLE BAND

Row 1: Ch 3, dc in each st across.

Row 2: Ch 1, sc across.

Fasten off.

INSTRUCTIONS

Turning chains: Begin each row of hdc with ch 2.

With White, ch 56.

Row 1 (RS): Hdc in 3rd ch from hk and in each ch across (54 sts).

Rows 2–30: Hdc in each hdc across (54 sts).

Rows 31–61: With White, work 12 hdc; work

Rows 62–91: With White, hdc in each hdc across.

Rows 92 and 93: Work Buttonhole Band.

FINISHING

Turn the piece over so the WS is facing up. Fold the bottom 10½ in / 27 cm up and the top 12 in / 30 cm down. The top should overlap the bottom by 2¾ in / 7 cm and the pillow should measure 20 in / 50 cm. Join the side edges with sc, working through all 3 layer where the top and bottom overlap on the back.

Sew 3 buttons onto the bottom, spacing evenly across. Use the spaces between the d stitches as buttonholes.

Weave in remaining ends.

BIG PERFORMANCE

THE RED CARPET IS SO YESTERDAY

SKILL LEVEL

Intermediate

FINISHED MEASUREMENTS:

Approx. 36 in / 90 cm diameter

MATERIALS

Yarn: Woll Butt Textilgarn 1 in/3 cm or equivalent (95% cotton, 5% other; 76 yd/ 69 m / 450 g)

Yarn Amounts:
Black, 2 cones
White, 2 cones

Hook: U.S. size N/P-15 / 10 mm

Notions: Tapestry needle

Gauge: 6 sc and 8 rows = 4 x 4 in / 10 x 10 cm in Fantasy Pattern. Adjust needle size to obtain correct gauge if necessary.

PATTERN STITCH

Work in the round, following instructions. Beginning on Rnd 8, watch the shape of the rug as you crochet. If the piece begins to ruffle up instead of lying flat, you have too many increases. Depending on your yarn and gauge, you may need to work rounds without increasing between the increase rounds.

INSTRUCTIONS

With White, make a magic ring.

Rnd 1: Ch 1 and work 10 sc into ring; join with sl st (10 sts).

Rnd 2: Ch 1, work 2 sc into each sc, join with sl st (20 sts).

Rnd 3 (Black): Ch 1, sc in first sc, *ch 2, sk next 2 sc, sc in next sc; rep from * 5 more times, sk next st, sc in first sc of rnd (there are now 2 sc in this space). Join with sl st.

Rnd 4 (White): Ch 1, sc in first st, *ch 3, sk the ch-sp, 2 sc in next sc; rep from * 5 more times, ch 2, sk last ch sp, sc in first sc (there are now 2 sc in this space). Join with sl st.

Rnd 5: Ch 1, sc in first sc, *ch 2, 2 sc in next ch sp, ch 2, 2 sc in next sc; rep from * 5 more times, ch 2, sc in first sc (there are now 2 sc in this space). Join with sl st.

Rnd 6 (Black): Ch 1, sc in first sc, *sc in next ch sp, 2 sc in next sc, rep from * 11 more times, sc in last ch sp, sc in first sc (there are now 2 sc in this space). Join with sl st (39 sts).

Rnd 7 (White): Ch 1, sc around, increasing 8 sts evenly spaced (47 sts).

Beginning with Rnd 8, increase at the same 8 points as needed to continue forming a circular shape. Rug should not ruffle up.

Rnds 8 and 9: Ch 1, sc around, join with sl st.

Rnd 10 (Black): Ch 1, sc around, join with sl st.

Rnds 11–13 (White): Ch 1, sc around, join with sl st.

Rnds 14 and 15 (Black): Ch 1, sc around, join with sl st.

Rnds 16–18 (White): Ch 1, sc around, join with sl st.

Rnds 19 and 20 (Black): Ch 1, sc around, join with sl st.

Rnds 21–23 (White): Ch 1, sc around, join with sl st.

Rnds 24 and 25 (Black): Ch 1, sc around, join with sl st.

Rnds 26–28 (White): Ch 1, sc around, join with sl st.

Rnd 29 (Black): Ch 1, sc around, join with sl st.

FINISHING

Weave in ends. Stretch rug to block, pinning onto a blocking surface. Spray to dampen and allow to dry thoroughly before unpinning.

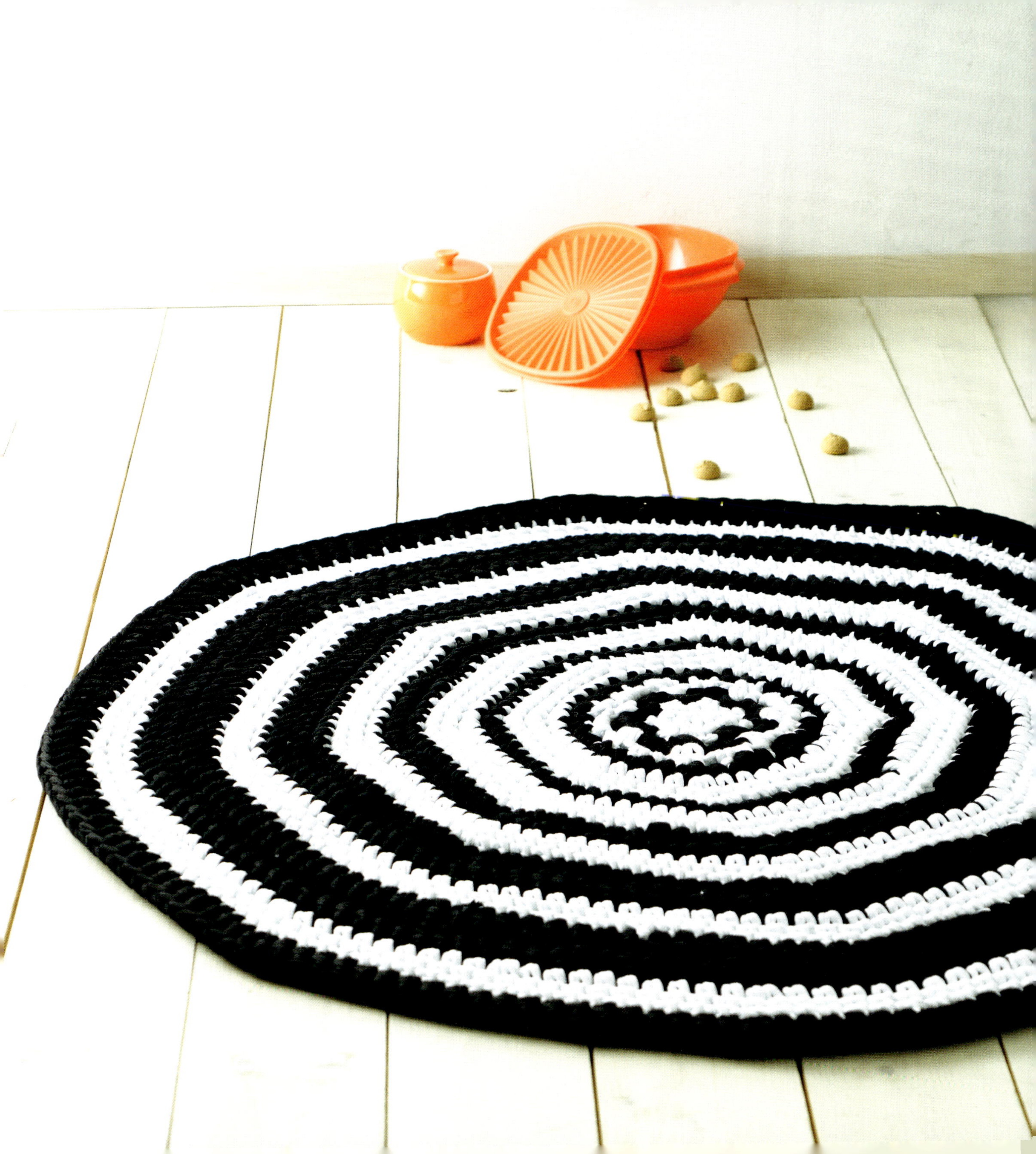

SHINE, SHINE

A TRENDY LAMPSHADE

SKILL LEVEL

Intermediate

FINISHED MEASUREMENTS:

Approx. 23 in / 59 cm in diameter, 14 in / 36 cm tall

MATERIALS

Yarn: CYCA #6 (super bulky/roving) Schachenmayr Bravo Big or equivalent (100% acrylic; 131 yd/120 m / 200 g)

Yarn Amounts:
White 101, 400 g
Black 199, 200 g

Hook: U.S. size M/N-13 / 9 mm

Notions: Tapestry needle, lampshade of matching dimensions, lamp

Gauge: 8 dc and 4 rows = 4 x 4 in / 10 x 10 cm. Adjust needle size to obtain correct gauge if necessary.

INSTRUCTIONS

With White, ch 162 and join with sl st.

Rnd 1 (White): Ch 2, hdc in each ch, join with sl st in the 2nd turning ch (162 sts).

Rnd 2 (White): Ch2, hdc in each hdc around, join with sl st.

Rnd 3 (White): Ch 4 (counts as tr), 1 tr, 2 dc, 3 hdc, 4 sc, 3 hdc, 3 dc, 2 tr, *2 tr, 3 dc, 3 hdc, 4 sc, 3 hdc, 3 dc, 2 tr; rep from * around, join with sl st in 4th turning ch.

Rnd 4 (Black): Ch 1, sc in each st around, join with sl st.

Rnd 5 (Black): Ch 1, 2 sc, 3 hdc, 2 dc, 4 tr, 3 dc, 3 hdc, 2 sc; from from * around, join with sl st.

Rnd 6 (Black): Ch3, dc in each st around, join with sl st.

Rnd 7 (Black): Rep Rnd 5.

Rnd 8 (White): Rep Rnd 4.

Rnd 9 (White): Rep Rnd 3.

Rnd 10 (White): Rep Rnd 6.

Rnd 11 (White): Rep Rnd 3.

Rnds 12–15 (Black): Rep Rnds 4–7.

Rnd 16 (White): Rep Rnd 4.

Rnd 17 (White): Rep Rnd 3.

Rnd 18 (White): Rep Rnd 6.

Rnd 19 (White): Rep Rnd 2.

Rnd 20 (White): Ch 1, (4 sc, sc2tog) around (135 sts).

Rnd 21 (White): Ch 1, (3 sc, sc2tog) around (108 sts).

FINISHING

Weave in ends. Use double sided tape to attach work to lampshade of matching dimensions, and then install in place on lamp.

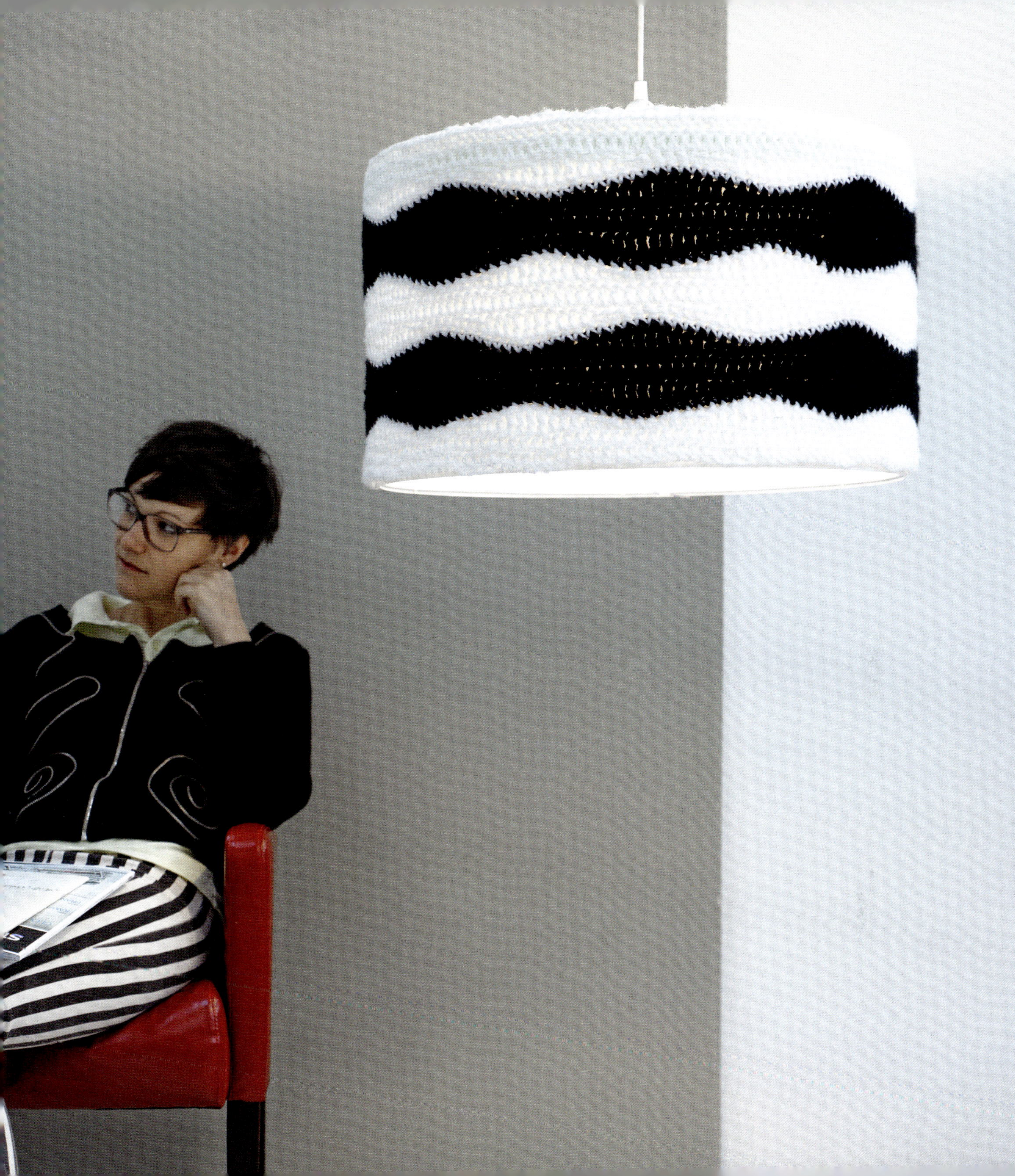

GREAT MOMENT

A SEAT CUSHION WITH REVERSE PATTERNING

SKILL LEVEL

Intermediate

FINISHED MEASUREMENTS:

Approx. 32 in / 80 cm

MATERIALS

Yarn: CYCA #6 (super bulky/roving) Schachenmayr Bravo Big or equivalent (100% acrylic; 131 yd/120 m / 200 g)

Yarn Amounts:
White #101, 800 g
Black #199, 800 g

Hook: U.S. size N/P-15 / 10 mm

Notions: Tapestry needle, 32 in / 80 cm pillow form

Gauge: 7 dc and 4½ rows = 4 x 4 in / 10 x 10 cm. Adjust needle size to obtain correct gauge if necessary.

PATTERN NOTES

The cushion is worked in the round with double crochet. Starting on Rnd 7, increases are worked with front-post double crochet at the color changes. Each rnd begins with 3 turning ch that counts as 1 dc, and ends by joining with a sl st to the 3rd ch.

INSTRUCTIONS

With Black, form a magic ring.

Rnd 1: Ch 3, 11 dc in magic ring, join with sl st (12 sts). Begin and end all other rnds the same way.

Rnd 2: Work 2 dc in each dc around (24 sts).

Rnd 3: *Dc in next dc, 2 dc in next dc; rep from * around (36 sts).

Rnd 4: *Dc in next 2 dc, 2 dc in next dc; rep from * around (48 sts).

Rnd 5: *Dc in next 3 dc, 2 dc in next dc; rep from * around (60 sts).

Rnd 6: 2 dc in first dc, dc in next 4 dc, *change to White, 2 dc in next dc, change to Black, 4 dc, 2 dc in next dc, 4 dc; from * to last 4 sts, and then, with Black, work 4 dc (72 sts).

Rnd 7: 5 dc, *change to White, FPdc in first White dc, dc in first White dc, dc in 2nd White dc, FPdc in 2nd White dc, change to Black, 10 dc; rep from * around to last 4 sts, and then, with Black, work 4 dc (84 sts).

Rnds 8–16: 5 dc, *change to White, FPdc in first White dc of group of White dc, dc in each White dc including last White dc, FPdc in last White dc of group of White dc, change to Black, 10 dc; rep from * around to last 4 sts, and then, with Black, work 4 dc.

Fasten off.

Make a second piece, reversing colors.

FINISHING

Weave in ends. Put pieces together with WS facing in. Sew halfway around, insert stuffing, and then sew the remaining portion closed.

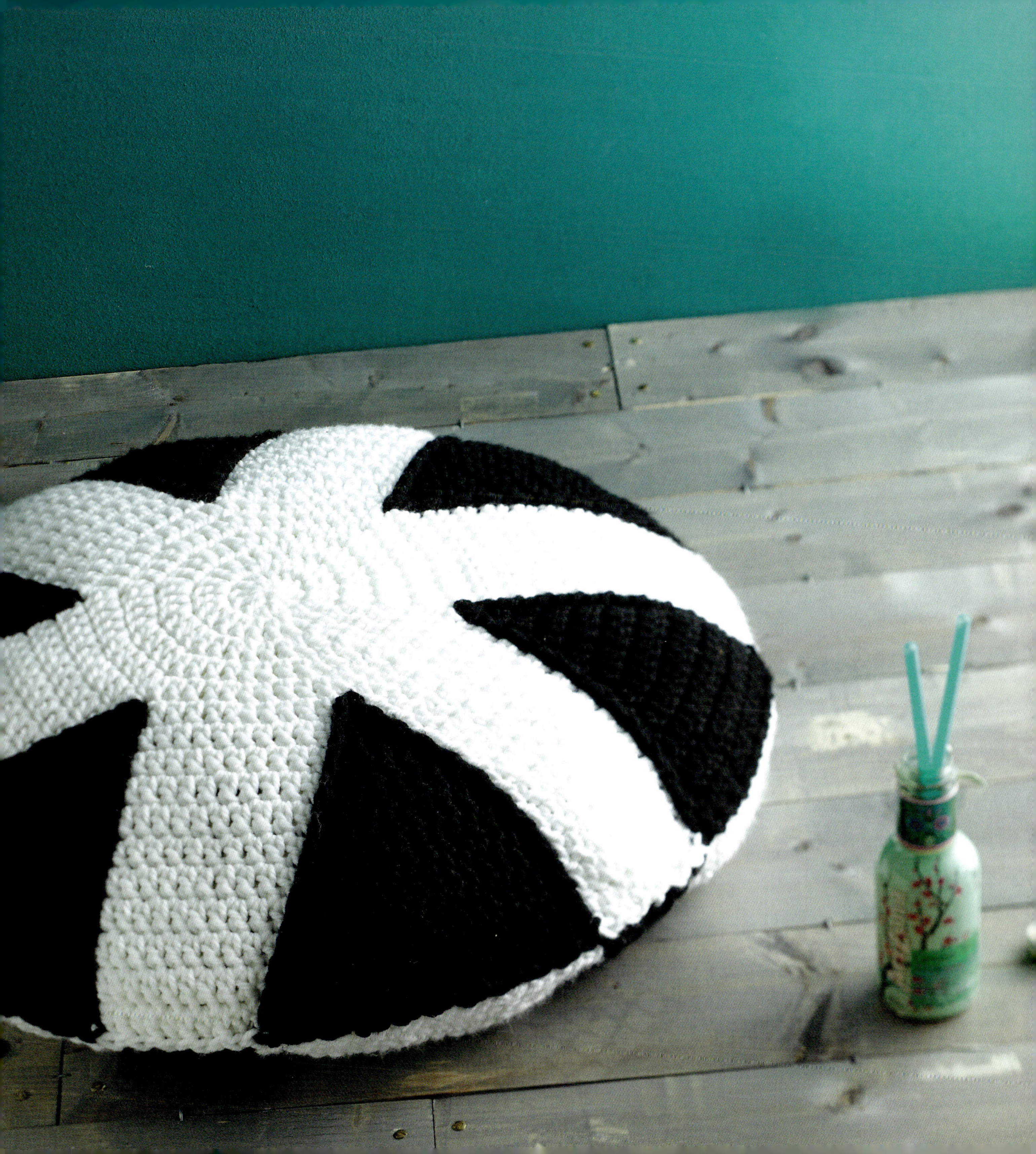

HAPPY SPIRAL

CUSHION WITH A WINDING PATTERN

SKILL LEVEL

Intermediate

FINISHED MEASUREMENTS:

Approx. 16 in / 40 cm

MATERIALS

Yarn: CYCA #6 (super bulky/roving) Schachenmayr Boston or equivalent (70% acrylic, 30% wool; 131 yd/120 m / 200 g)

Yarn Amounts:
White #101, 200 g
Black #99, 200 g

Hook: U.S. size K-10½ / 7 mm

Notions: Tapestry needle, 16 in / 40 cm pillow form, removable stitch marker

Gauge: 12 dc and 5 rows = 4 x 4 in / 10 x 10 cm. Adjust needle size to obtain correct gauge if necessary.

INSTRUCTIONS

Cushion is worked in spiral rounds. With White, form a magic ring.

Rnd 1: Ch 1, work 1 hdc and 3 dc in magic ring. Pull the loop on the hook to enlarge it and set it aside to be worked later. With Black, ch 1 and work 4 dc in the magic ring and contract the ring. Place markers to indicate the beginning of the rnd for both colors.

Rnd 2: Continuing with Black, work 2 sc in the White hdc and in each of the 3 White dc. Pull the Black loop on the hook to enlarge it and set it aside to be worked later. Put the White loop back on the hook and work 2 dc in each of the 5 Black sc.

Rnd 3: Continuing with White, * 2 dc in the next Black sc, dc in next st; rep from * 3 more times. Set the White loop aside and put the Black loop back on the hook, * 2 sc in the next 2 White dc, sc in the next st; rep from * 3 more times.

Rnds 4–6: In each of the doubled White dc sts in the previous rnd, work 2 Black sc and in each plain White dc, work 1 Black sc. In each of the doubled Black sc of the previous round, work 2 White dc and in each plain Black sc, work 1 White dc (increases worked in the same places as on the previous rnd).

Rnds 7 and 8: For a smooth outer edge, work with no additional increases. Piece should measure approx. 15¾ in / 40 cm in diameter. End the White section with 1 hdc, 1 sc, and 1 sl st. End the Black section with 1 sl st. Fasten off.

Make a second piece the same way, reversing colors.

FINISHING

Weave in ends. Put pieces together with WS facing in. Sew halfway around, insert stuffing, and then sew the remaining portion closed.

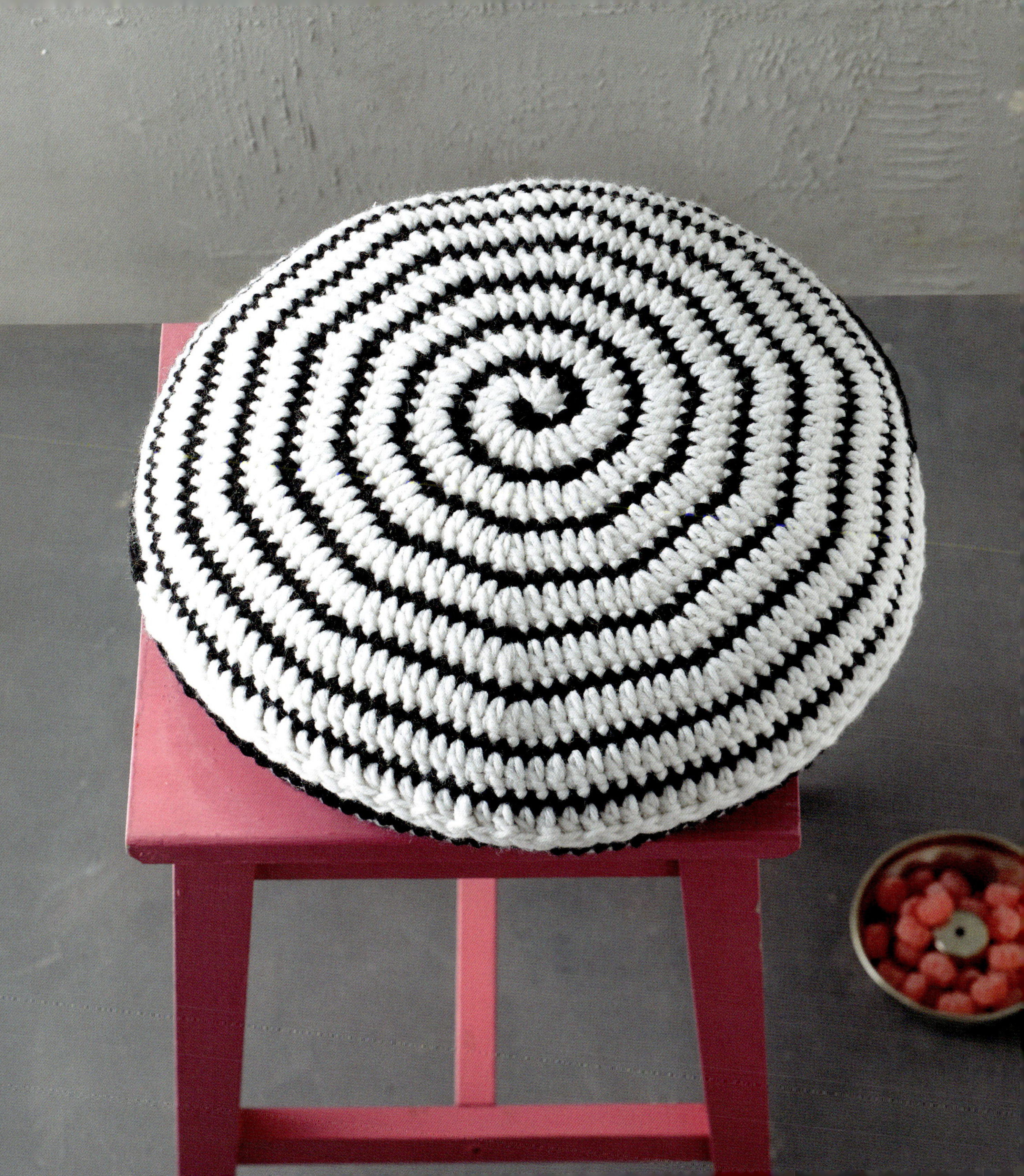

SKILL LEVEL

Easy

FINISHED MEASUREMENTS:

Approx. 28 x 40 in / 70 x 100 cm

MATERIALS

Yarn: CYCA #6 (super bulky/roving) Schachenmayr Boston or equivalent (131 yd/120 m / 200 g)

Yarn Amounts:
White #101, 500 g
Black #99, 250 g

Hook: U.S. size 7 / 4.5 mm

Notions: Tapestry needle, 28 x 40 in / 70 x 100 cm wooden frame

Gauge: 3 hdc and 8 rows = 4 x 4 in / 10 x 10 cm. Adjust needle size to obtain correct gauge if necessary.

Chart: Page 94

INSTRUCTIONS

Mural is worked in rows with hdc throughout.
With White, ch 122.

Row 1 (White): Hdc in 3rd ch from hk and each ch across (120 sts).

Rows 2 and 3 (White): Ch 2, hdc across.

Rows 4–32 (White): Ch 2, 6 hdc, work next 108 sts as charted, 6 hdc.

Rows 33–52 (White): Rep Row 2.

FINISHING

Embroider the outline of the buildings with White, using the photo as a guide. Weave in ends. Stretch mural to fit over wooden frame and use staple gun to secure in place.

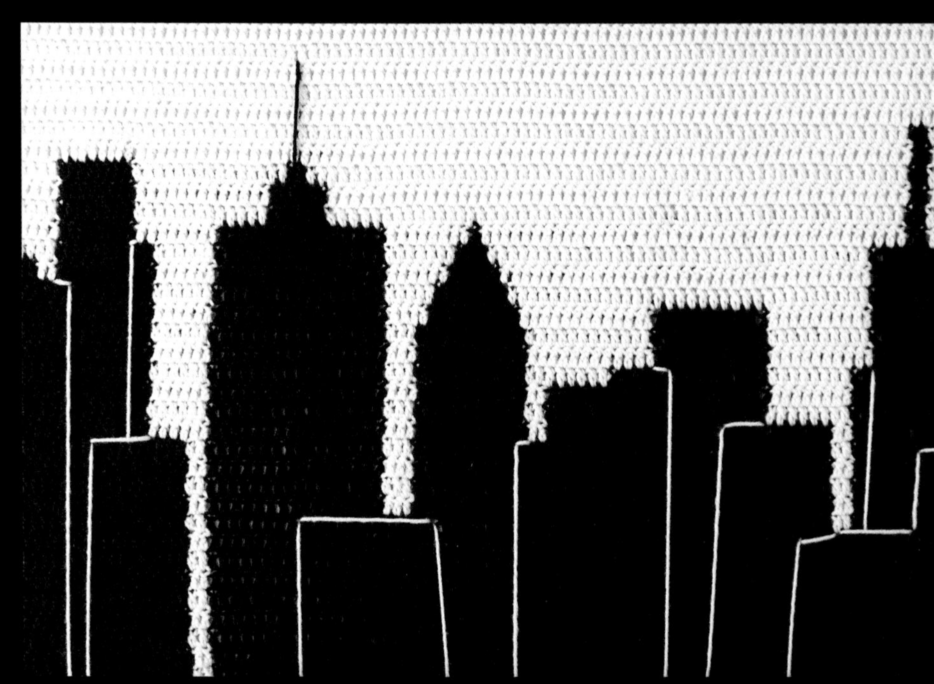

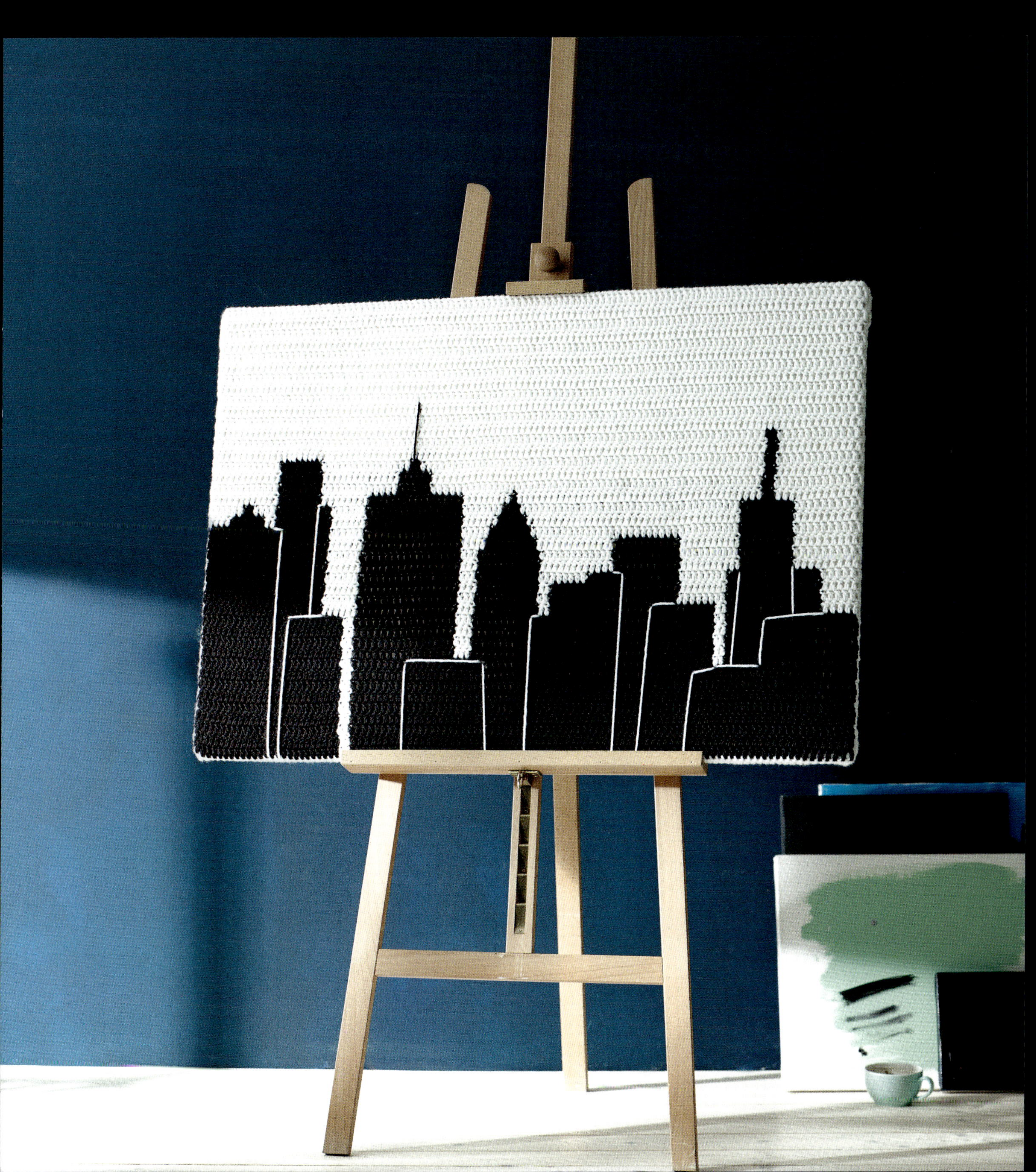

ALL ABOUT STYLE

STYLISH CUSHION TRIO

SKILL LEVEL

Easy

FINISHED MEASUREMENTS:

Approx. 16 x 28 in / 40 x 70 cm

MATERIALS

Yarn: CYCA #6 (super bulky/roving) Schachenmayr Boston or equivalent (131 yd/ 120 m / 200 g)

Yarn Amounts:
White #101, 400 g
Black #99, 50 g

Hook: U.S. size 7 / 4.5 mm

Notions: Tapestry needle, 16 x 28 in / 40 x 70 cm pillow form

Gauge: 13 hdc and 8 rows = 4 x 4 in / 10 x 10 cm. Adjust needle size to obtain correct gauge if necessary.

Chart(s): Pages 96 and 97

INSTRUCTIONS

MUSTACHE CUSHION

With White, ch 48.

Row 1: Hdc in 3rd ch from hk and in each ch across (46 sts).

Rows 2–34 (White): Ch 2, hdc in each hdc across (46 sts).

Rows 35–75 (White): Ch 2, 17 hdc, work next 11 sts as charted, 18 hdc.

Rows 76–110 (White): Ch 2, hdc in each hdc across (46 sts).

Fasten off.

BOWTIE CUSHION

With White, ch 48.

Row 1: Hdc in 3rd ch from hk and in each ch across (46 sts).

Rows 2–34 (White): Ch 2, hdc in each hdc across (46 sts).

Rows 35–75 (White): Ch 2, 10 hdc, work next 25 sts as charted, 11 hdc.

Rows 76–110 (White): Ch 2, hdc in each hdc across (46 sts).

Fasten off.

SUNGLASS CUSHION

With White, ch 48.

Row 1: Hdc in 3rd ch from hk and in each ch across (46 sts).

Rows 2–34 (White): Ch 2, hdc in each hdc across (46 sts).

Rows 35–75 (White): Ch 2, 12 hdc, work next 22 sts as charted, 12 hdc.

Rows 76–110 (White): Ch 2, hdc in each hdc across (46 sts).

Fasten off.

FINISHING

Weave in ends.

Turn in the long ends so they overlap about 2 in / 5 cm in the center. Sew the sides. Insert the cushion.

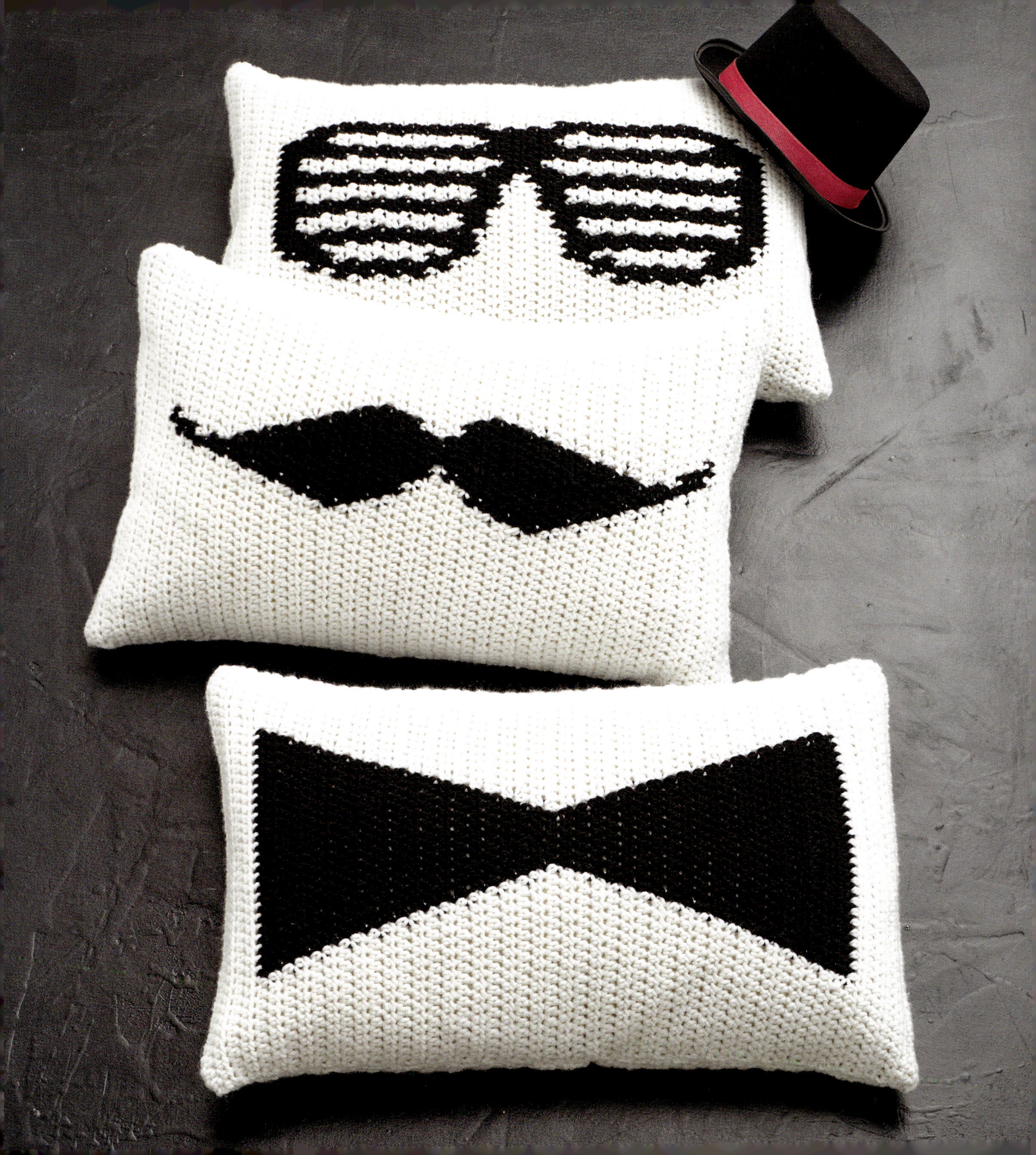

LABYRINTH

WINDING DOOR MAT

LABRYNTH PATTERN

Mat is crocheted in rows from the center out. Each row starts with 1 turning ch. Each new strip is begun with 1 turning chain then single crochet sts worked along the short end of the previous strips. See diagram for arrangement of strips.

INSTRUCTIONS

BLACK STRIP 1

Ch 21.

Row 1: Sc in 2nd ch from hook and each ch across (20 sts).

Rows 2 and 3: Ch 1, sc in each sc across (20 sts).

Pull the loop on the hook to enlarge it and set it aside to be worked later.

WHITE STRIP 1

Work on the other side of the foundation chain.

Row 1: Join the yarn to the first Black ch. Ch 1, sc in each sc across (20 sts).

Rows 2 and 3: Ch 1, sc in each sc across (20 sts.)

WHITE STRIP 2

Rotate the work 90 degrees to the right (clockwise), ch 1, sc across short end of White Strip 1 (3 st), then sc across short end of Black Strip 1 (6 sts total).

Pull the loop on the hook to enlarge it and set it aside to be worked later.

BLACK STRIP 2

Put the Black loop back on the hook, rotate the work 90 degrees to the right and work as for White Strip 2.

Pull the loop on the hook to enlarge it and set it aside to be worked later.

WHITE STRIP 3

Put the White loop back on the hook. Rotate the work 90 degrees to the right.

Row 1: Ch 1, work 3 sc across short end of White Strip, then work 20 sc across the long edge of the Black Strip, then work 3 sc across the short end of the White Strip (26 sts).

Rows 2 and 3: Ch 1, sc in each sc across (26 sts).

Pull the loop on the hook to enlarge it and set it aside to be worked later.

BLACK STRIP 3

Put the Black loop back on the hook, rotate the work 90 degrees to the right and work as for White Strip 3.

Continue to work additional strips in this fashion (see diagram) until the mat is the desired size. The sample has 17 strips.

FINISHING

Weave in ends.

Wash and dry flat to block if desired.

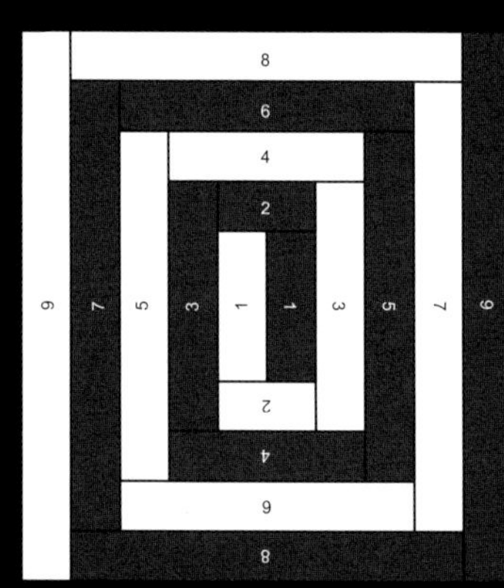

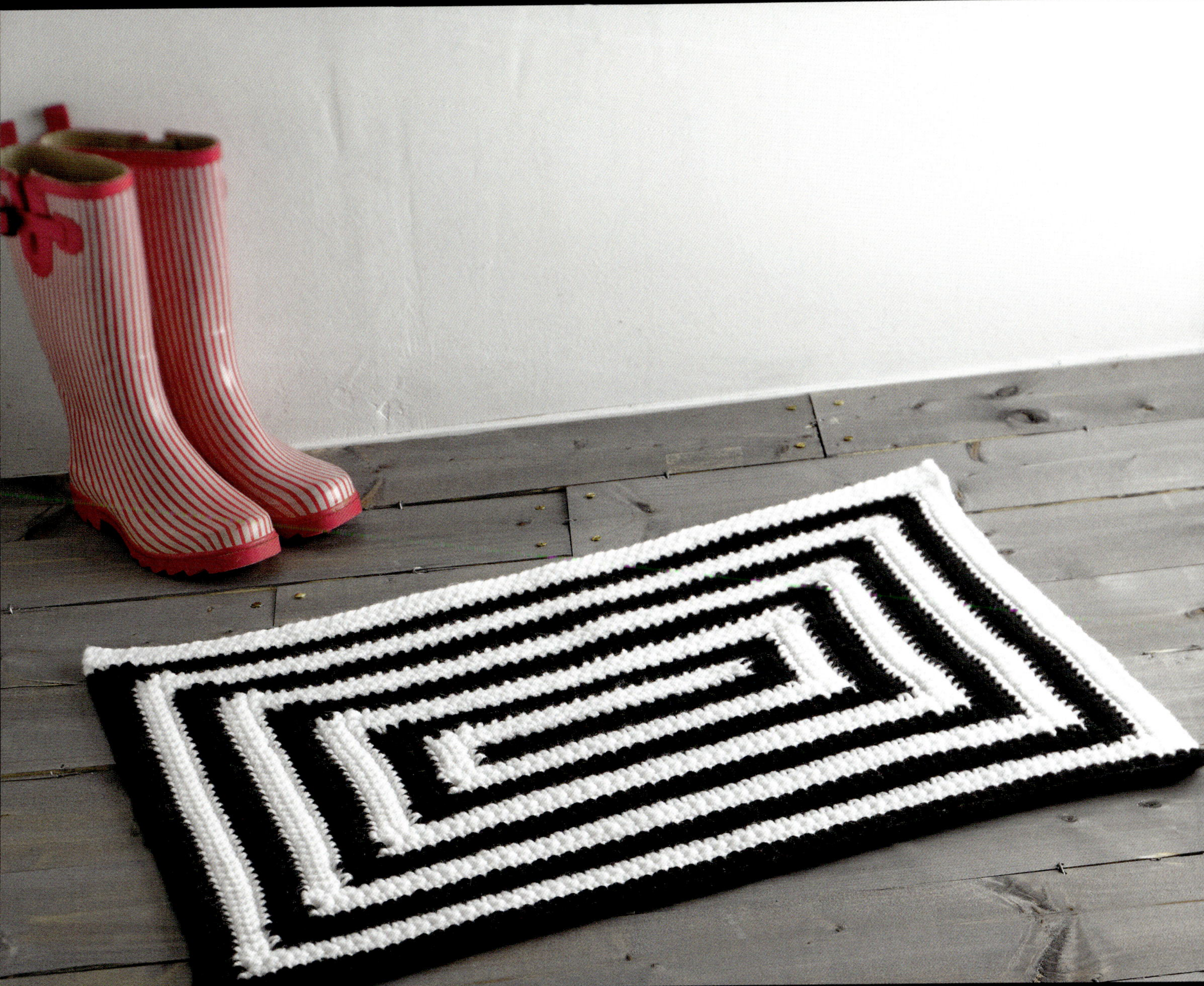

SKILL LEVEL

Intermediate

FINISHED MEASUREMENTS:

Approx. 22 x 29 in / 56 x 74 cm

MATERIALS

Yarn: CYCA #6 (super bulky/roving) Schachenmayr Bravo Big or equivalent (131 yd/120 m / 200 g)

Yarn Amounts:
White #101, 400 g
Black #199, 400 g

Hook: U.S. size L-11 / 8 mm

Notions: Tapestry needle

Gauge: 9 sc and 10 rows = 4 x 4 in / 10 x 10 cm. Adjust needle size to obtain correct gauge if necessary.

PLANTING FUN

A CROCHET FLOWER POT

SKILL LEVEL

Intermediate

FINISHED MEASUREMENTS:

Approx. 9 in / 23 cm diameter and 8 in / 20 cm tall

MATERIALS

Yarn: CYCA #6 (super bulky/roving) Schachenmayr Merino Super Big Mix (87 yd/ 80 m / 100g)

Yarn Amounts:
Black #99, 200 g
White #101, 100 g

Hook: U.S. size K-10½ / 7 mm

Notions: Tapestry needle

Gauge: 13 dc and 7 rows = 4 x 4 in / 10 x 10 cm. Adjust needle size to obtain correct gauge if necessary.

PINEAPPLE STITCH

Rnd 1 (Black): Ch 1, insert hk into the next st and draw up a lp, yo hk, insert hk into next st and draw up a lp, draw yarn through all 3 lps on hk, ch 1, * insert hk into the same st as the previous st and draw up a lp, yo hk, insert hk into next st and draw up a lp, draw yarn through all 3 lps on hk, ch 1; rep from * around. Join with sl st to first ch.

Rnd 2 (White): Ch 1, * insert hk into next ch sp of prev rnd and draw up a lp, yo hk, insert hk into next ch sp and draw up a lp, draw yarn through all 3 lps on hk, ch 1; rep from * around. Join with sl st in first ch.

Rep Rnd 2 for pattern.

INSTRUCTIONS

Pot is worked in the round. Each rnd begins with ch 3, which counts as 1 dc. Each rnd ends by joining with a sl st to the 3rd ch.

With Black, form a magic ring.

Rnd 1: Ch 3, 8 dc in magic ring, join with sl st to 3rd ch (9 sts). Begin and end each following rnd the same way unless otherwise indicated.

Rnd 2: 2 dc in each dc around (18 sts).

Rnd 3: (Dc in next dc, 2 dc in next dc) around (27 sts).

Rnd 4: (Dc in next 2 dc, 2 dc in next dc) around (36 sts).

Rnd 5: (Dc in next 3 dc, 2 dc in next dc) around (45 sts).

Rnd 6: (Dc in next 4 dc, 2 dc in next dc) around (54 sts).

Rnd 7: (Dc in next 5 dc, 2 dc in next dc) around (63 sts).

Rnd 8: (Dc in next 6 dc, 2 dc in next dc) around (72 sts).

Rnd 9: (Dc in next 7 dc, 2 dc in next dc) around (81 sts).

Rnd 10: Ch 1, sc in each dc around, join with sl st (81 sts).

Rnds 11–26: Work in Pineapple Stitch, switching colors after each rnd.

Rnds 27–29: With Black, work in Pineapple Stitch.

FINISHING

Work 1 rnd of crab stitch. Fasten off. Weave in ends.

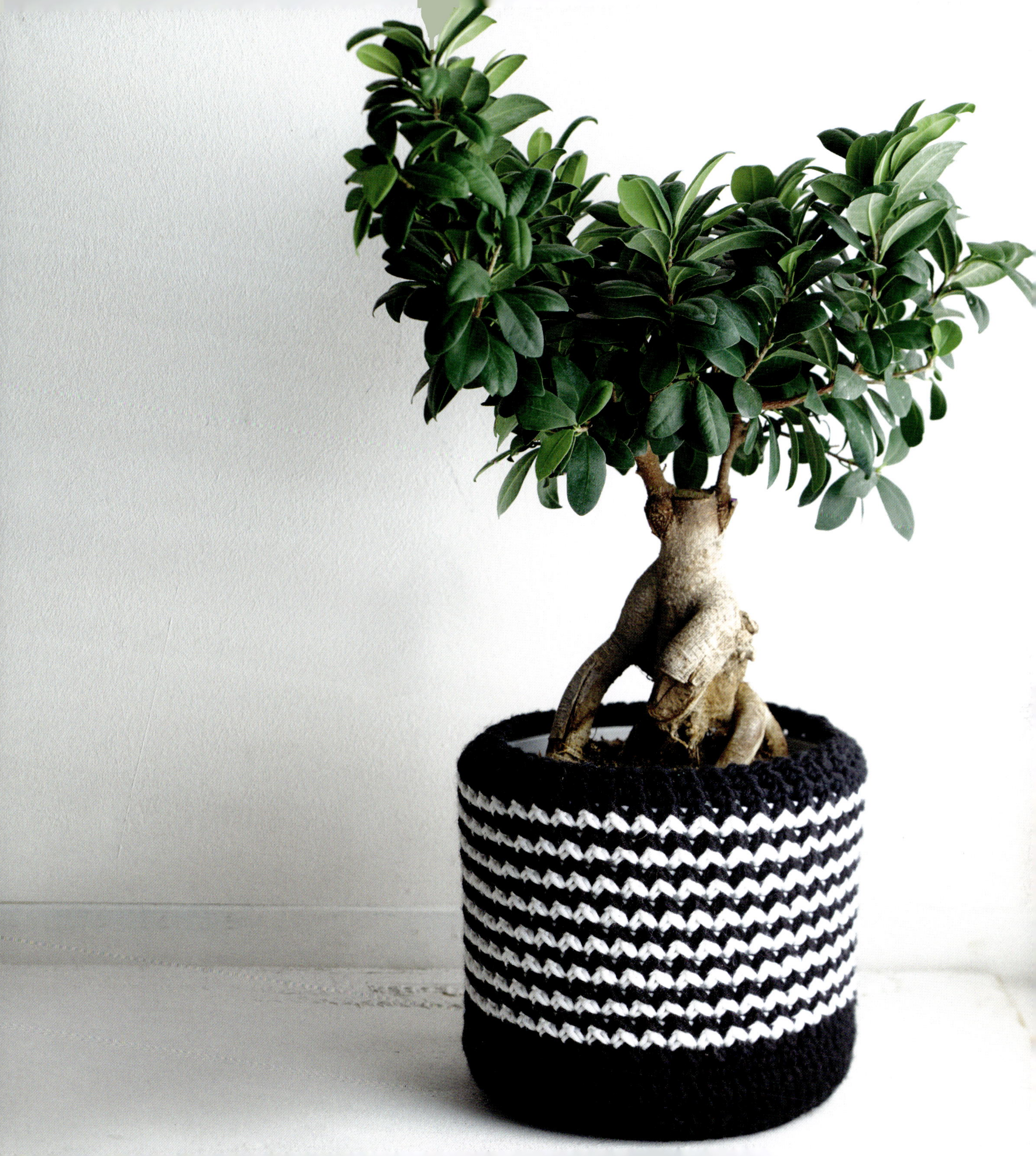

IN THE MOOD FOR LOVE

STRIPED HEARTS

SKILL LEVEL

Easy

FINISHED MEASUREMENTS:

5 in / 13 cm high, 3¾ in / 9.5 cm wide

MATERIALS

Yarn: CYCA #4 (worsted/afghan/aran), Schachenmayr Catania Grande or equivalent (100% cotton; 68 yd/62 m / 50 g)

Yarn Amounts:
Black #3110, 25 g
White #3106, 25 g

Hook: U.S. size G-6 / 4 mm

Notions: Tapestry needle, fiber fill stuffing

Gauge: 18 sc and 18 rows = 4 x 4 in / 10 x 10 cm. Adjust needle size to obtain correct gauge if necessary.

INSTRUCTIONS

The hearts are worked in the round using sc. Each rnd begins with ch 1 and ends with a sl st to the beg ch. The curved sections at the top of the heart are worked separately and then joined together. Starting at Rnd 8, fill with stuffing as you go.

TOP CURVE

With Black, form a magic ring.

Rnd 1 (Black): Ch 1, 8 sc in magic ring, and join with sl st (8 sts). Begin and end all other rnds the same way.

Rnd 2 (Black): 2 sc in each sc around (16 sts).

Rnds 3 and 4 (Black): Sc in each sc around.

Rnd 5 (White): Sc in each sc around.

Cut yarn. Make a second piece the same way. Place the two pieces so the yarn tails are close together and the pieces are touching.

BOTTOM TRIANGLE

Rejoin the yarn to the outer edge of the heart.

Rnd 1 (White): Ch 1, sc in each sc across the front half of the first Top Curve, switch to the second Top Curve and sc in each sc around, switch to the back half of the first Top Curve and sc in each sc to beg of rnd. Join with sl st in turning ch (32 sts). Begin and end all other rnds the same way.

Rnd 2: (White): Sc in each sc around.

Rnd 3 (Black): Sc in each sc around.

Rnd 4 (Black): (6 sc, sc2tog) around (28 sts).

Rnd 5 (Black): Sc in each sc around.

Rnd 6 (White): (5 sc, sc2tog) around (24 sts).

Rnd 7 (White): Sc in each sc around.

Rnd 8 (White): (4 sc, sc2tog) around (20 sts).

Rnd 9 (Black): Sc in each sc around.

Rnd 10 (Black): (3 sc, sc2tog) around (16 sts).

Rnd 11 (Black): Sc in each sc around.

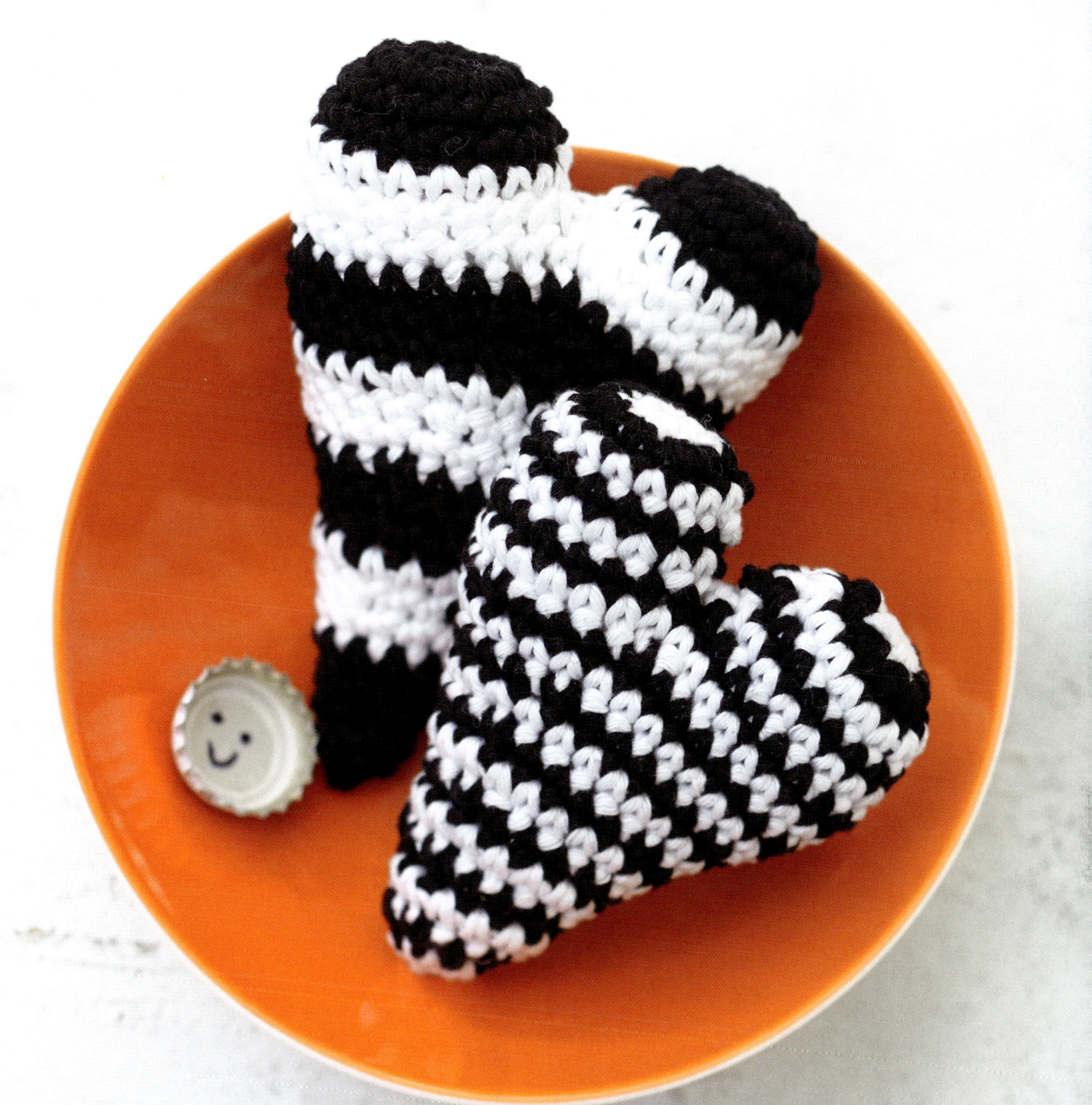

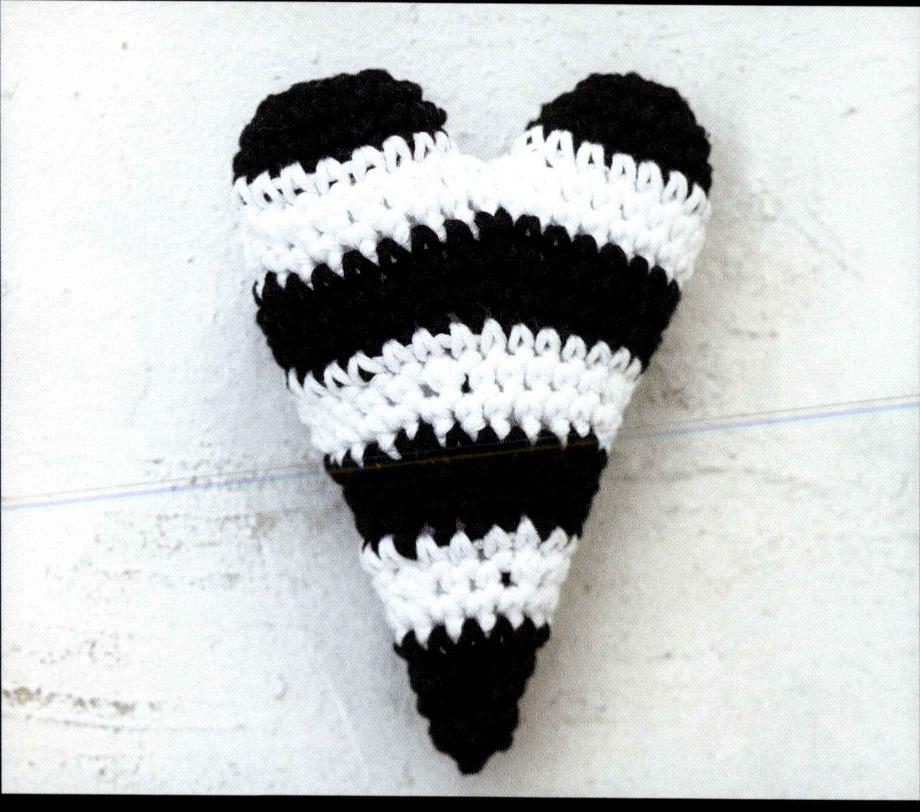

Rnd 12 (White): (2 sc, sc2tog) around (12 sts).

Rnd 13 (White): Sc in each sc around.

Rnd 14 (White): (Sc, sc2tog) around (8 sts).

Rnd 15 (Black): Sc in each sc around.

Rnd 16 (Black): (Sc2tog) around (4 sts).

Sc through both layers to close bottom.

FINISHING

Weave in ends.

VARIATION

Work as for the 2-row stripe heart, but begin with White and change colors every rnd.

PRACTICAL SQUARES

MITERED-SQUARE TABLE RUNNER

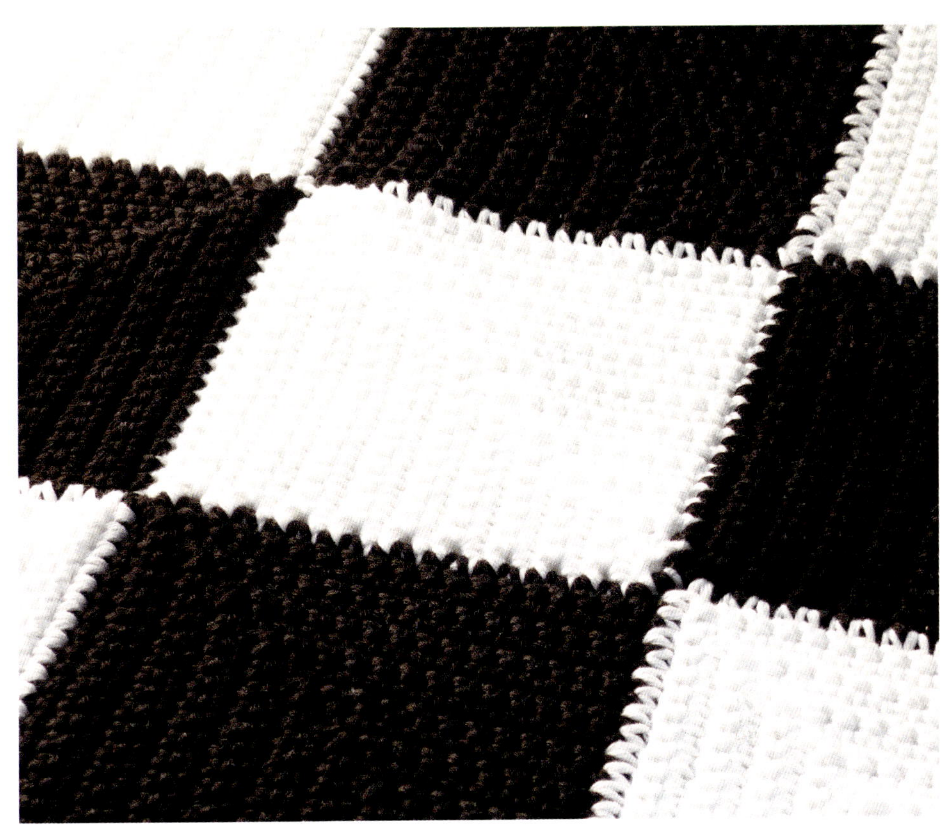

SKILL LEVEL

Intermediate

FINISHED MEASUREMENTS:

40 in / 102 cm by 13½ in / 34 cm

MATERIALS

Yarn: CYCA #4 (worsted/afghan/aran), Schachenmayr Catania Grande or equivalent (100% cotton; 68 yd/62 m / 50 g)

Yarn Amounts:
White #3106, 150 6
Black #3110, 50 g

Hook: U.S. size G-6 / 4 mm

Notions: Tapestry needle

Gauge: 18 sc and 18 rows = 4 x 4 in / 10 x 10 cm. Adjust needle size to obtain correct gauge if necessary.

Chart(s): Page 98

MITERED SQUARES

The mitered squares are worked in rows with sc. Each row begins with 1 turning ch. The squares are worked attached to one another.

INSTRUCTIONS

SQUARE 1: WHITE

With White, ch 22.

Row 1: Sc in 2nd ch from hook and next 8 ch. Insert hk into next ch and draw up a lp, yo hk, sk 1 ch, insert hk in to the next ch and draw up a lp, draw yarn through all 3 lps on hk. Sc in in each ch to end (19 sts).

Row 2: Ch 1 (turning ch; begin all following rows the same way). 8 sc, *insert hk into next sc and draw up a lp, sk next sc (corner), insert hk into next sc and draw up a lp, draw yarn through all 3 lps on hk, sc in each sc to end* (17 sts).

Row 3: 7 sc; rep from * to * (15 sts).

Row 4: 6 sc; rep from * to * (13 sts).

Row 5: 5 sc; rep from * to * (11 sts).

Row 6: 4 sc; rep from * to * (9 sts).

Row 7: 3 sc; rep from * to * (7 sts).

Row 8: 2 sc; rep from * to * (5 sts).

Row 9: 1 sc; rep from * to * (3 sts).

Row 10: Insert hk into first sc and draw up a lp, sk next sc, insert hk into next sc and draw up a lp, draw yarn through all 3 lps on hk. Fasten off and cut yarn.

SQUARE 2: BLACK

Join Black to the bottom right corner of the White square just completed. Ch 12. Sc in 2nd ch from hook and in the next 8 ch. Insert hk into next ch and draw up a lp, sk next ch (corner) and draw up a lp, insert hk into first sc on White square and draw up a lp, yo hook and draw through all 3 lps. Work 9 sc across side of White square. Turn and work Rows 2–10 as for Square 1.

SQUARE 3: WHITE

Join White to the top left corner of the White square and work as for Square 2.

Work remaining squares as for Square 2, following the schematic on page 98 as a guide for placement—27 squares total.

FINISHING

Weave in ends.

Wash and dry flat to block, then iron on WS if desired.

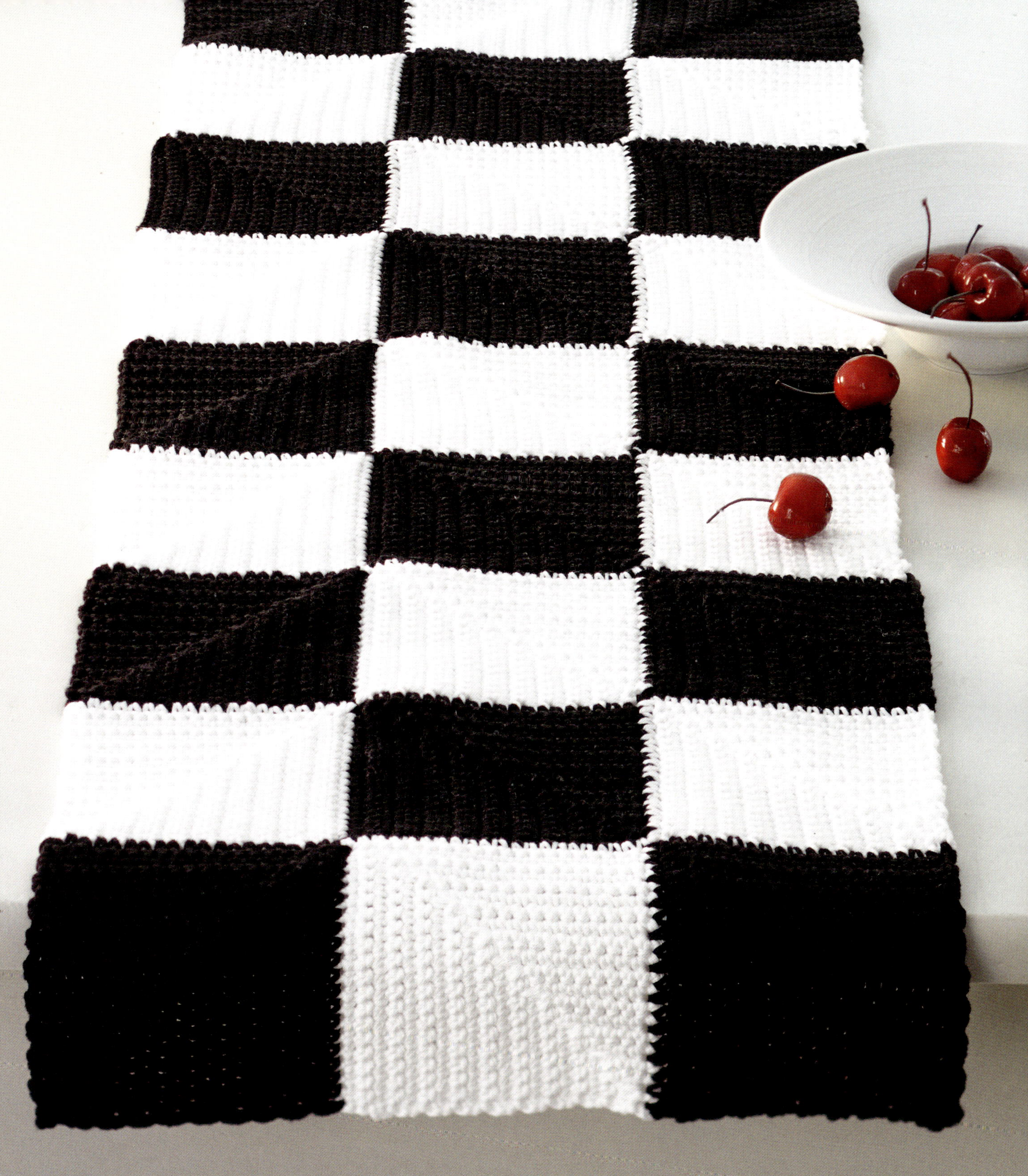

CHIC IN CROCHET

STRIPED VASE COVERS

SKILL LEVEL

Easy

FINISHED MEASUREMENTS:

12½ in / 32 cm high, to fit 15 in / 38.5 cm vase

MATERIALS

Yarn: CYCA #6 (super bulky/roving) Schachenmayr Bravo Big or equivalent (131 yd/120 m / 200 g)

Yarn Amounts:
Black #199, 100 g
White #101, 100 g

Hook: U.S. size K-10½ / 7 mm

Notions: Tapestry needle, stitch marker, 1 liter glass vase

Gauge: 8 sc and 9 rows = 4 x 4 in / 10 x 10 cm. Adjust needle size to obtain correct gauge if necessary.

INSTRUCTIONS

Vase is worked in spiral rnds. Use a marker and move it up at the beg of each rnd.

With White, ch 30. Join with sl st to form a ring.

Rnds 1–4 (White): Sc in each ch around (30 sts).

Rnds 5–7 (Black): Sc in each sc around.

Rnds 8–10 (White): Sc in each sc around.

Rnds 11–13 (Black): Sc in each sc around.

Rnds 14 and 15 (White): Sc in each sc around.

Rnd 16 (White): (Sc in next sc, sc2tog) around (20 sts).

Rnd 17 (Black): Sc in each sc around.

Rnd 18 (Black): Sc in first sc, *sc2tog, sc in next sc; rep from * 5 more times, sc in last sc (14 sts).

Rnd 19 (Black): Sc in each sc around.

Rnds 20–22 (White): Sc in each sc around.

Rnds 23–25 (Black): Sc in each sc around.

Rnds 26 and 27 (White): Sc in each sc around.

Rnd 28 (White): (Sc in next st, 2 sc in next st) around (21 sts).

Rnd 29 (White): Sc in each sc around.

FINISHING

Weave in ends. Insert vase into cover.

VARIATION

Work vase with Black and make three White stripes on Rnds 5, 8, and 11.

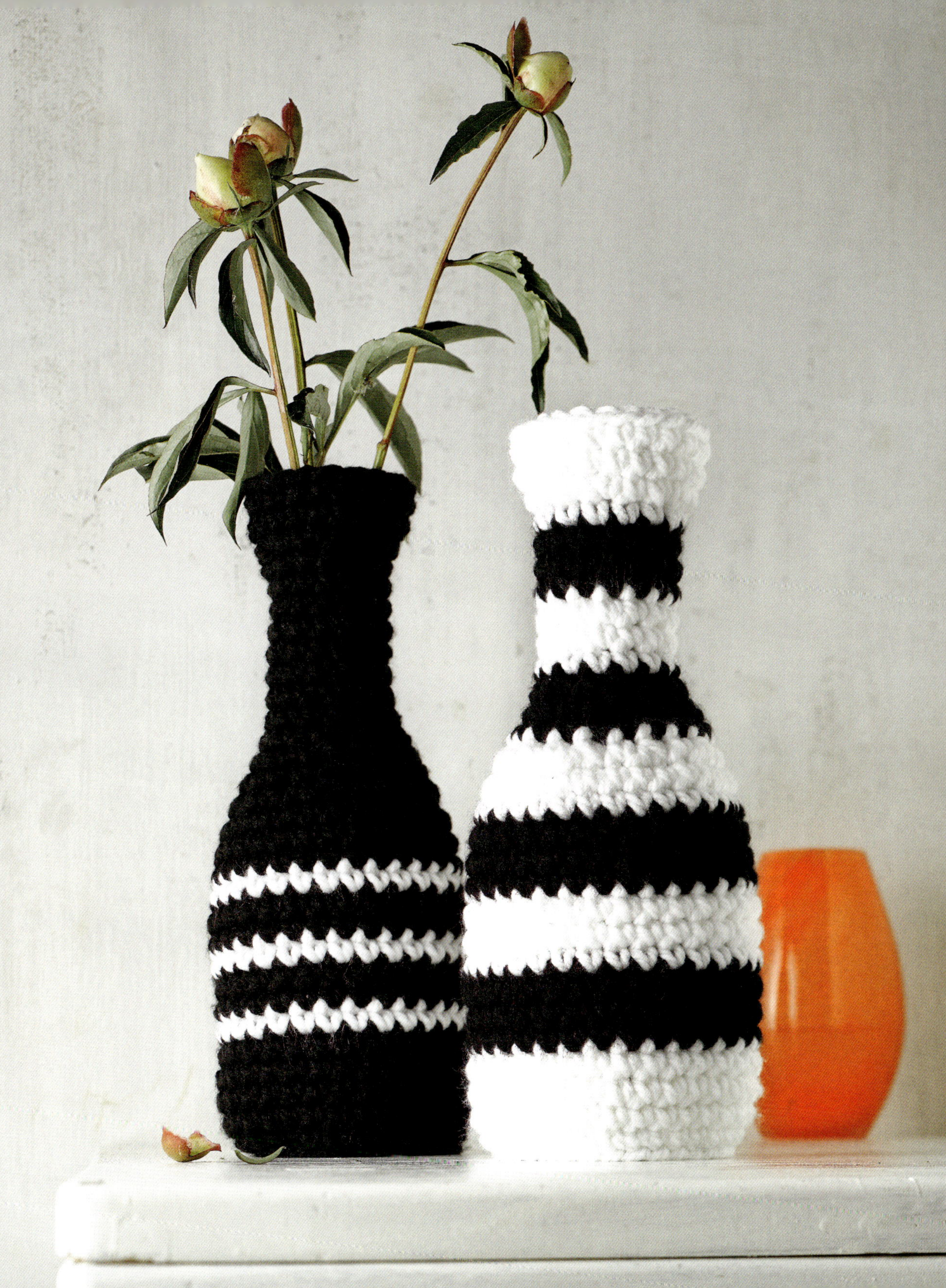

SKILL LEVEL

Experienced

FINISHED MEASUREMENTS:

2¾ in / 7 cm tall, 2 in / 5 cm diameter

MATERIALS

Yarn: CYCA #3 (DK/light worsted), Schachenmayr Catania or equivalent (100% cotton; 137 yd/125 m / 50 g)

Yarn Amounts: Small amounts of White #106 and Black #110

Hook: U.S. size C-2 or D-3 / 3 mm

Notions: Tapestry needle, 4 glass candle holders 2 in / 5 cm in diameter

Gauge: 19 dc and 10 rows = 4 x 4 in / 10 x 10 cm. Adjust needle size to obtain correct gauge if necessary.

BOBBLE

Yo hk, insert hk into next st and draw up a lp, yo hk, insert hk into same st and draw up a lp, yo hk and draw yarn through all 5 lps on hk.

BOBBLE CANDLE SHADE

With White, ch 36 and join with sl st to form a ring.

Rnd 1 (White): Ch 1, sc in each ch around, join with sl st (36 sts).

Rnd 2 (Black): Ch 1, sc in back lp of each sc around, join with sl st.

Rnd 3 (White): Ch 2, dc in first st (counts as 1 bobble), ch 2, make bobble in next st, * sk 2 sts, make bobble in next st; rep from * 8 more times, sk the last 2 sts, then sl st to first dc of rnd.

Rnd 4 (Black): Ch 1, sc in the sl st from the prev rnd, ch 3, sc between the 2nd and 3rd bobbles, ch 3; *skip the next 2 bobbles and sc between the following 2 bobbles, ch 3; rep from * 7 more times. Join with sl st.

Rnd 5 (White): In the first ch sp, [ch 2, dc, ch 2, make bobble], * in the next ch sp, [make bobble, ch 2, make bobble]; rep from * 7 more times. Join with sl st.

Rnd 6 (Black): Rep Rnd 4.

Rnds 7–11: Change colors and rep Rnds 4 and 5.

Rnd 12 (Black): Ch 1, sc in back lp of each sc around. Join with sl st.

Rnd 13 (White): Ch 1, sc in back lp of each sc around. Join with sl st.

WAVE CANDLE SHADE

With White, ch 36 and join with sl st to form a ring.

Rnd 1 (White): Ch 1, sc in each ch around, join with sl st (36 sts).

Rnd 2 (Black): Ch 1, sc in back lp of each sc around. Join with sl st.

Rnd 3 (White): Ch 3 (turning ch), ch 1, dc in next st, sk next 2 sts, *in next st [dc, ch1, dc], sk next 2 sts; rep from * 11 more times. End rnd with sl st in 3rd turning ch. Work another sl st in the ch sp.

Rnd 4 (Black): In the first ch sp [ch 3 (turning ch), ch1, dc], *in the next ch sp [dc, ch1, dc]; rep from * 11 more times. Join with sl st in 3rd turning ch. Work another sl st in the ch sp.

Rnds 5–10: Changing colors, rep Rnds 3 and 4.

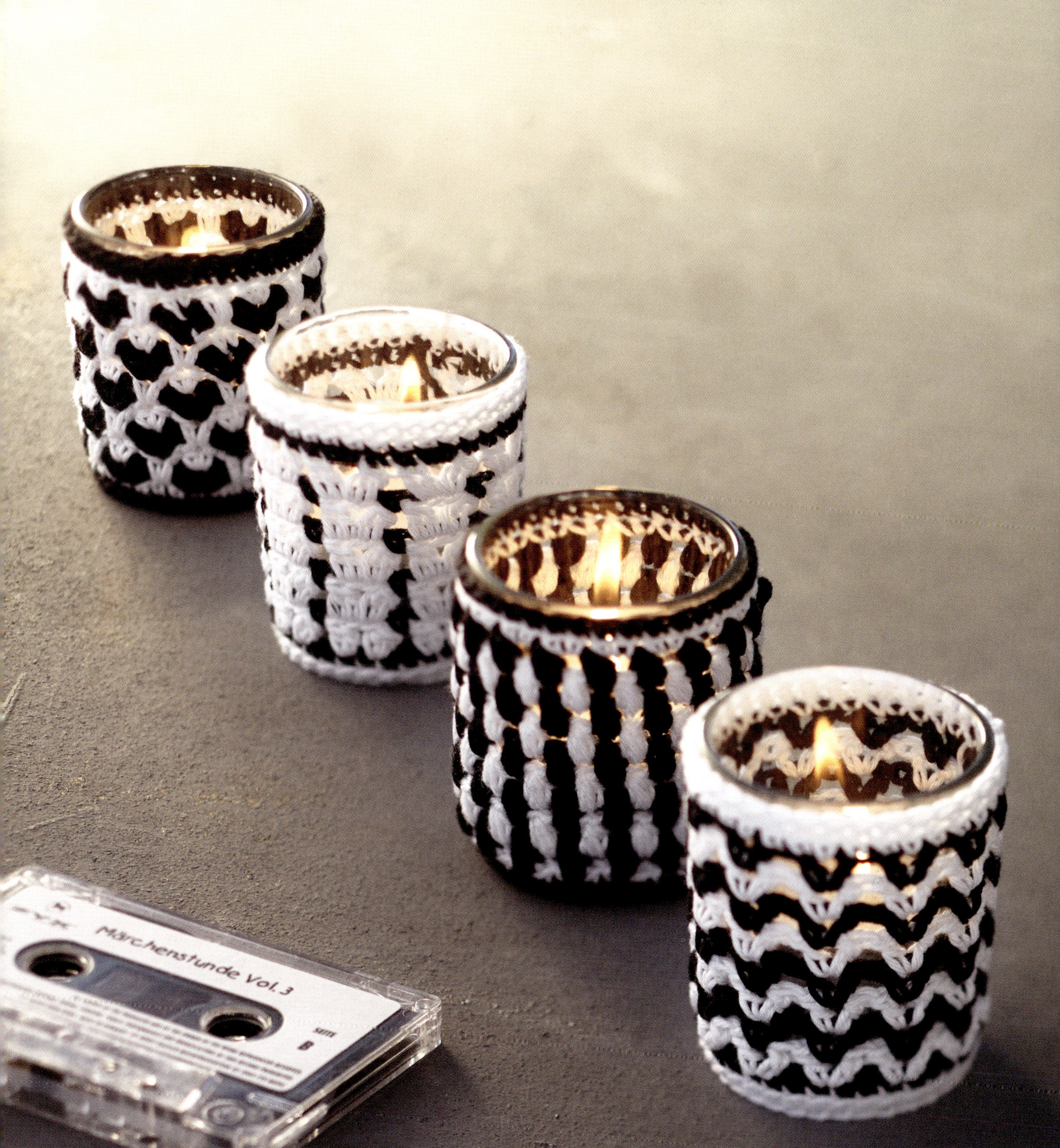
Märchenstunde Vol. 3

Rnds 11 and 12 (White): Sc in back lp of each sc around. Join with sl st.

SHELL CANDLE SHADE

With Black, ch 36 and join with sl st to form a ring.

Rnd 1 (Black): Ch 1, sc in each ch around, join with sl st (36 sts).

Rnd 2 (White): Ch 1, sc in back lp of each sc around, join with sl st.

Rnd 3 (Black): Ch 3 and 3 dc in first st (first shell), sk next 3 sts, * 4 dc in the next st (second shell), sk next 3 sts; rep from * 8 more times. End rnd with sl st in 3rd turning ch. Work another sl st between the next 2 dc.

Rnd 4 (White): Ch 2, hdc between 2nd and 3rd dc of 1st shell, 2 dc in the sc of Rnd 2 between 1st and 2nd shells, * 2 hdc between the 2nd and 3rd dc of the next shell, 2 dc in the sc of Rnd 2 between the next 2 fans; rep from * 8 more times. Join with sl st in the first hdc. Work another sl st between the next 2 dc.

Rnd 5 (Black): Ch 3 and 3 dc between the next 2 dc of the prev rnd, * 4 dc between the next 2 dc of the prev rnd; rep from * 8 more times.

Rnd 6: Rep rnd 4.

Rnds 7–12: Change colors and rep Rnds 4 and 5.

Rnds 13 and 14 (Black): Ch 1, sc in back lp of each sc around, join with sl st.

BASKETWEAVE CANDLE SHADE

With Black, ch 36 and join with sl st to form a ring.

Rnd 1 (Black): Ch 1, sc in each ch around, join with sl st—36 sc.

Rnd 2 (White): Ch 1, sc in back lp of each sc around, join with sl st.

Rnd 3 (Black): Ch 2, hdc, ch1, sk next st, * make bobble in next st, ch 1, sk next st; rep from * around (18 bobbles). Join with sl st in 1st hdc. Work another sl st between 1st and 2nd bobbles.

Rnd 4 (White): Ch 1, hdc and ch 1 in next ch, sk next bobble, * ch 1, make bobble in next ch, sk next bobble; rep from * around (18 bobbles). Join with sl st in 1st hdc.

Rnds 5–11: Change colors and rep Rnds 3 and 4.

Rnd 12 (White): Ch 1, 2 sc in each ch on prev rnd, join with sl st—36 sts.

Rnd 13 (Black): Ch 1, sc in back lp of each sc around, join with sl st.

FINISHING (FOR ALL CANDLE SHADES)

Weave in ends.

PAINT IT BLACK

WALL HANGINGS WITH A MODERN LOOK

SKILL LEVEL

Easy

FINISHED MEASUREMENTS:

12 x 12 in / 30 x 30 cm

MATERIALS

Yarn: CYCA #4 (worsted/afghan/aran), Schachenmayr Catania Grande or equivalent (100% cotton; 68 yd/62 m / 50 g)

Yarn Amounts:
Black #3110, 450 g
White #3106, 150 g

Hook: U.S. size G-6 / 4 mm

Notions: Tapestry needle, 3 wooden frames 12 x 12 in / 30 x 30 cm, staple gun

Gauge: 18 sc and 18 rows = 4 x 4 in / 10 x 10 cm. Adjust needle size to obtain correct gauge if necessary.

Chart(s): Page 98

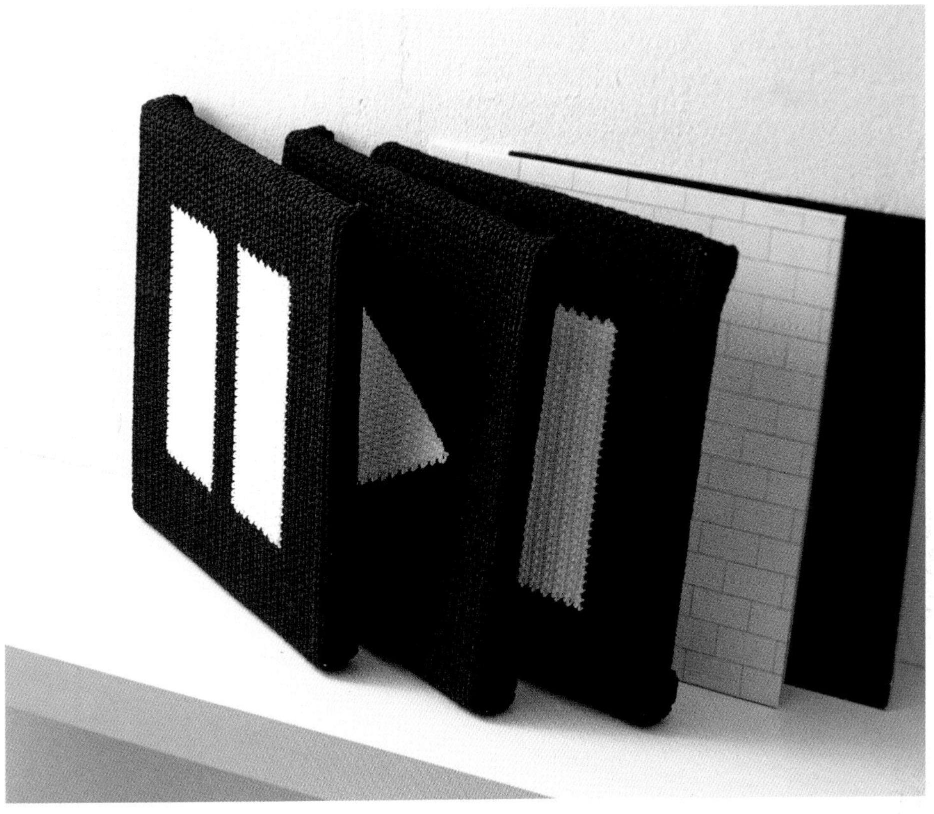

INSTRUCTIONS

Worked back and forth in rows. Begin every row after Row 1 with ch 1 (turning ch).

STOP

With Black, ch 65.

Row 1 (Black): Sc in 2nd ch from hk and in each ch across (64 sts).

Rows 2–18 (Black): Sc in each sc across.

Rows 19–52: With Black, work 16 sc; with White, work 32 sc; with Black, work 16 sc.

Rows 53–70 (Black): Sc in each sc across.

PAUSE

With Black, ch 65.

Rows 2–18 (Black): Sc in each sc across.

Rows 19–32: With Black, work 16 sc; with White, work 32 sc; with Black, work 16 sc.

Rows 33–38 (Black): Sc in each sc across.

Rows 39–52: With Black, work 16 sc; with White, work 32 sc; with Black, work 16 sc.

Rows 53–70 (Black): Sc in each sc across.

PLAY

Rows 2–18 (Black): Sc in each sc across.

Rows 19–51: With Black, work 15 sc; work chart across next 33 sts; with Black, work 16 sc.

Rows 52–70 (Black): Sc in each sc across.

FINISHING

Weave in ends. Stretch the crochet pieces over the wooden frames and staple gun in place.

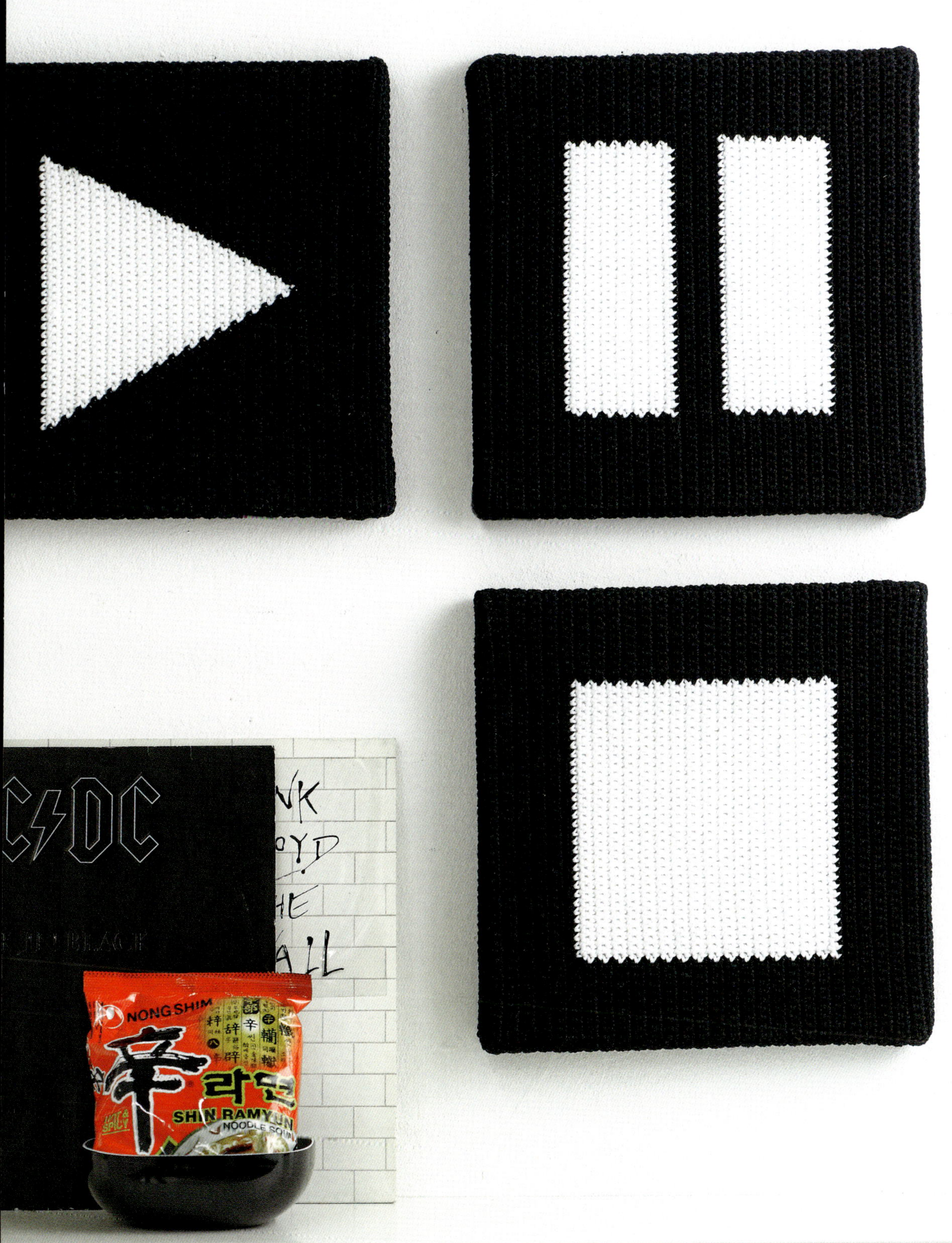
NONG SHIM
라면
SHIN RAMYUN

JUST FOR FUN

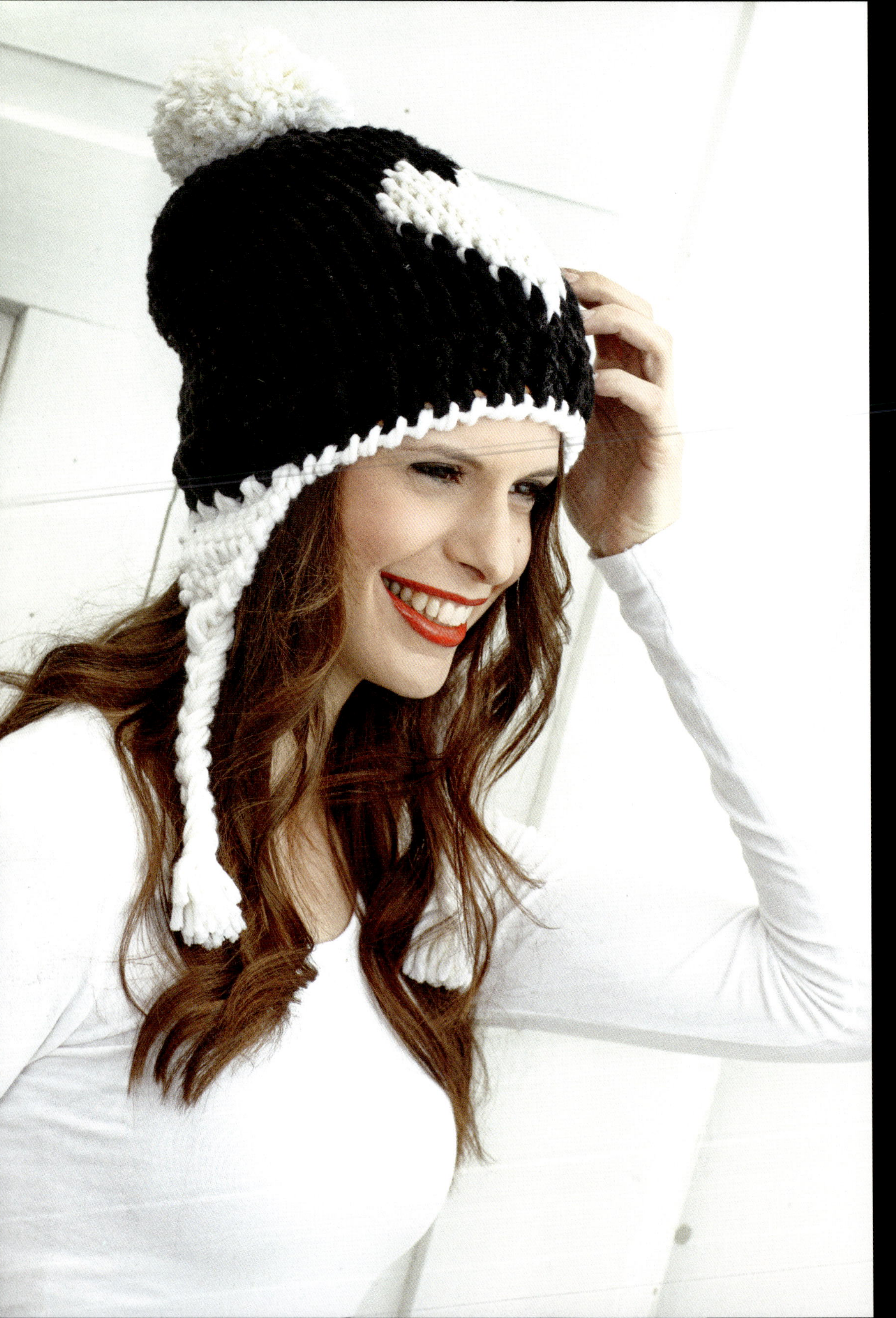

SKILL LEVEL

Experienced

FINISHED MEASUREMENTS:

To fit head 20½ to 22 in / 52 to 56 cm around

MATERIALS

Yarn: CYCA #6 (super bulky/ roving) Schachenmayr Merino Extrafine 40 (100% merino; 43 yd/39 m / 50g)

Yarn Amounts:
Black #399, 200 g
White #301, 50 g

Hook: U.S. size K-10½ / 7 mm

Notions: Tapestry needle

Gauge: 12 sts and 10 rows = 4 x 4 in / 10 x 10 cm in Front-Post Double Crochet. Adjust needle size to obtain correct gauge if necessary.

Chart: Page 98

HEART OVER HEAD

HAT WITH EAR FLAPS

RIBBING

The hat brim is worked in Front Post Double Crochet and hdc in rnds beginning with ch 2 (turning ch) and ending with a sl st to join.

FRONT POST DOUBLE CROCHET (FPDC)

The hat body is worked in Front Post Double Crochet in rnds beginning with ch 3 (turning ch, counts as 1 dc) and ending with a sl st to join.

INSTRUCTIONS

With Black, ch 46 and join with sl st to form a ring.

Rnd 1 (Black): Ch 2, hdc in each ch across (46 hdc).

Rnds 2 and 3 (Black): Ch 1, * fpdc in next st, hdc in next st; rep from * around and join with sl st.

Rnd 4 (Black): Ch 3, (fpdc in next 5 sts, 2 fpdc in next st) around, join with sl st (53 sts).

Rnds 5–13: With Black, ch 3, 20 fpdc; work chart over next 13 sts; with Black, 20 fpdc, join with sl st.

Rnds 14–16 (Black): Ch 3, fpdc in each st

EAR FLAPS

Place a marker at the center back of the hat. For the left ear flap, join White in the 5th st from the marker. Work back and forth in rows.

Row 1: Ch 3, 9 dc.

Row 2: Ch 3, 8 dc.

Row 3: Ch 3, 7 dc.

Row 4: Ch 3, 6 dc.

Fasten off and cut yarn.

Make right ear flap in the same way on the other side of the center back marker.

FINISHING

With White, work 1 row of crab stitch around

HEARTBREAKERS

CUFFS WITH A MESSAGE

SKILL LEVEL

Intermediate

FINISHED MEASUREMENTS:

Width at bottom 4¾ in / 12 cm, width at top 4 in / 10 cm, length 9 in / 23 cm

MATERIALS

Yarn: CYCA #6 (super bulky/roving) Schachenmayr Merino Extrafine 40 (100% merino; 43 yd/39 m / 50g)

Yarn Amounts:
Black #399, 200 g
White #301, 50 g

Hook: U.S. size K-10½ / 7 mm

Notions: Tapestry needle

Gauge: 12 sts and 10 rows = 4 x 4 in / 10 x 10 cm in Front Post Double Crochet. Adjust needle size to obtain correct gauge if necessary.

INSTRUCTIONS

With Black, ch 24 and join with sl st to form a ring.

Rnd 1 (Black): Ch 3, dc in each ch around, join with sl st (24 sts).

Rnds 2–6 (Black): Ch 3, fpdc around, join with sl st.

Rnd 7 (Black): Fpdc around to last 2 sts, fpdc2tog (23 sts).

Rnd 8 (Black): Rep Rnd 7 (22 sts).

Rnd 9 (Black): Rep Rnd 7 (21 sts).

Rnds 10–15: With Black, ch 3, 6 fpdc; work chart over next 8 sts; with Black, 6 fpdc, join with sl st.

THUMB OPENING (RIGHT CUFF)

Rnd 16: Work patts as set and after working the chart, sk 2 sts, ch 4, and work as set to end of rnd.

THUMB OPENING (LEFT CUFF)

Rnd 16: Work patts as set to 2 sts before chart, sk 2 sts, ch 4, and work as set to end of rnd.

BOTH CUFFS

Rnd 17: Work patts as set and work 2 dc over ch sp.

Rnd 18: Rep Rnd 15.

Rnds 19 and 20 (Black): Ch 3, fpdc around, join with sl st.

FINISHING

Weave in ends.

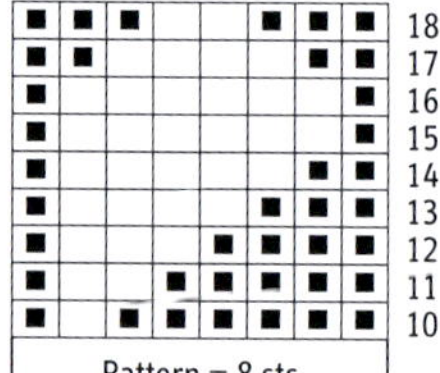

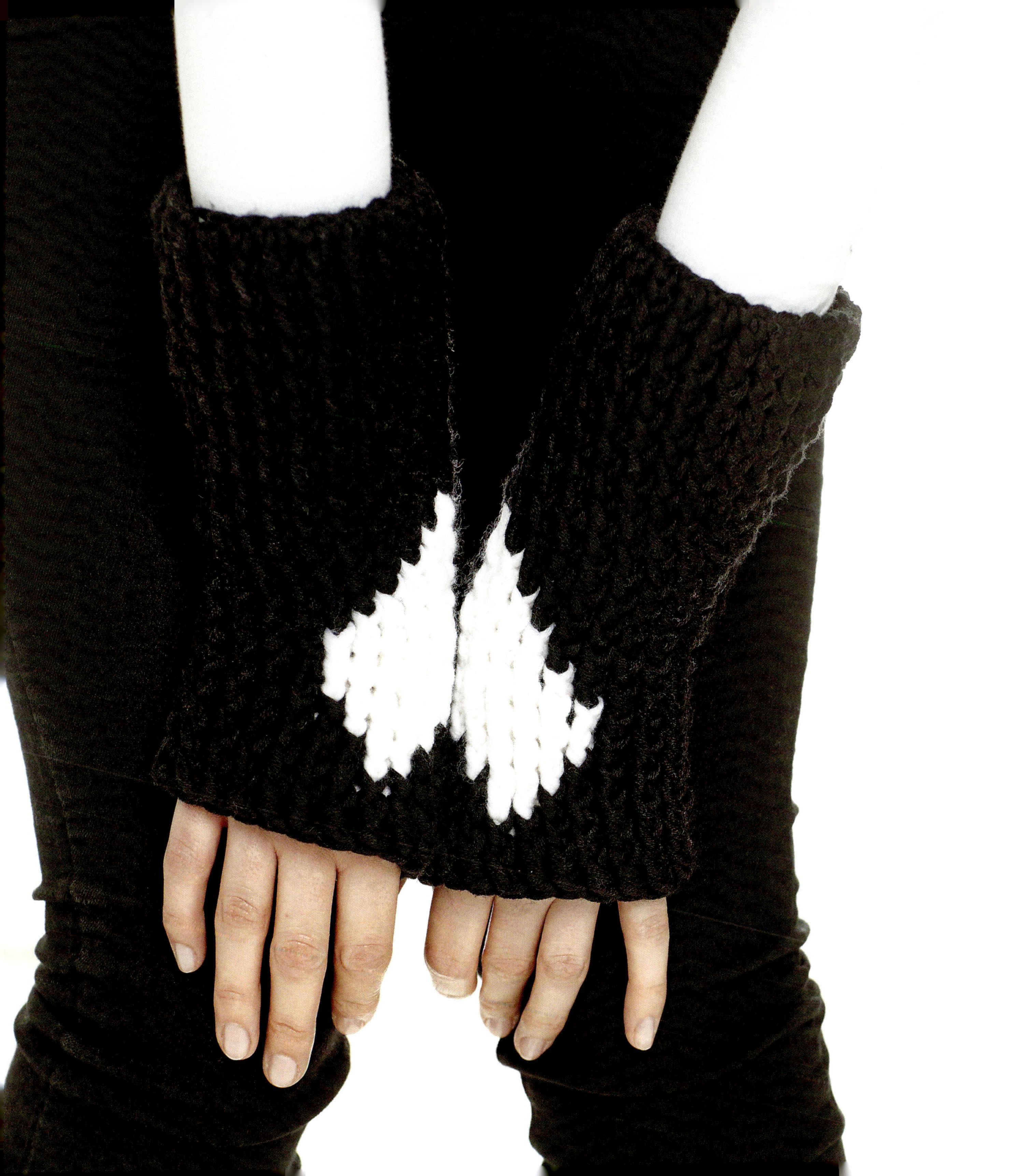

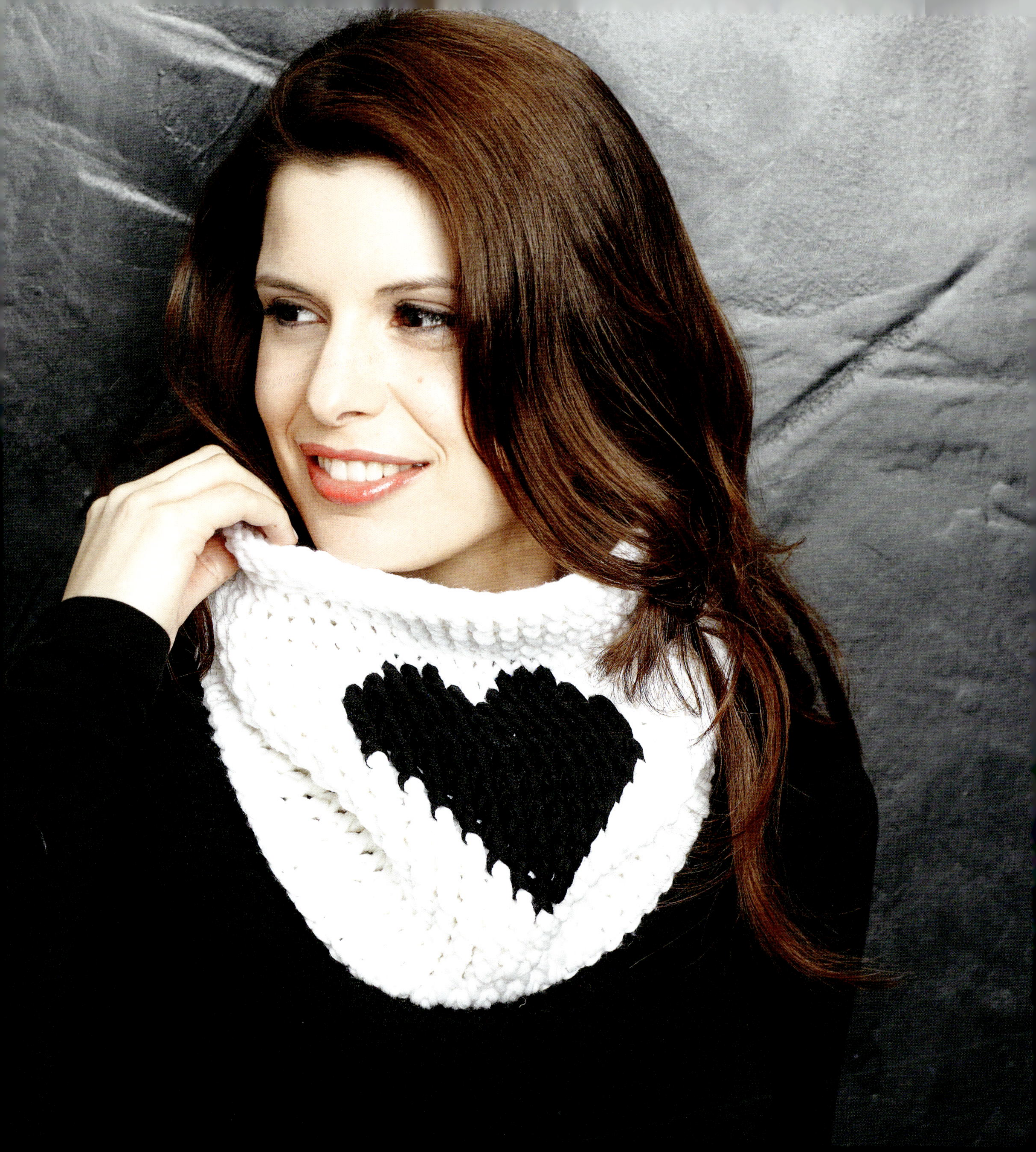

CLOSE TO MY HEART

CLASSIC COWL WITH HEART

SKILL LEVEL

Intermediate

FINISHED MEASUREMENTS:

Width 10 in / 30 cm, length 12 in / 25 cm

MATERIALS

Yarn: CYCA #6 (super bulky/roving) Schachenmayr Merino Extrafine 40 (100% merino; 43 yd/39 m / 50g)

Yarn Amounts:
White #301, 250 g
Black #399, 50 g

Hook: U.S. size M/N-13 / 9 mm

Notions: Tapestry needle

Gauge: 10 sts and 8 rows = 4 x 4 in / 10 x 10 cm in Front Post Double Crochet. Adjust needle size to obtain correct gauge if necessary.

Chart: Page 98

INSTRUCTIONS

With White, ch 60 and join with sl st to form a ring.

Rnd 1 (White): Ch 3, dc in each ch around, join with sl st (60 sts).

Rnds 2–4 (White): Ch 3, fpdc in each dc around, join with sl st.

Rnds 5–15: With White, ch 3, 22 fpdc; work chart over next 15 sts; with White, 22 fpdc, join with sl st.

Rnds 16–21 (White): Ch 3, fpdc in each dc around, join with sl st.

FINISHING

Weave in ends.

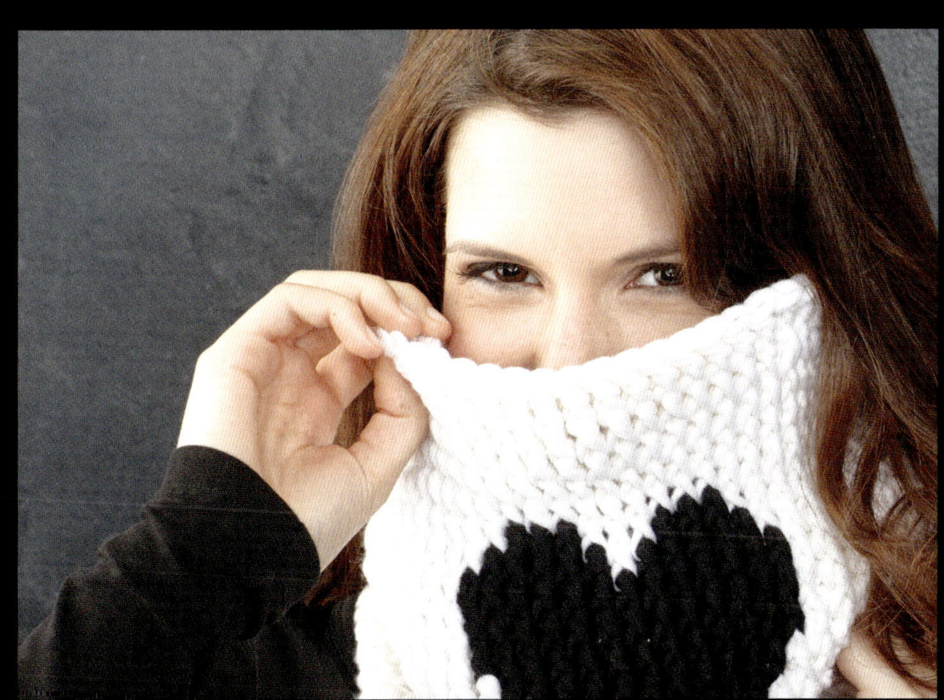

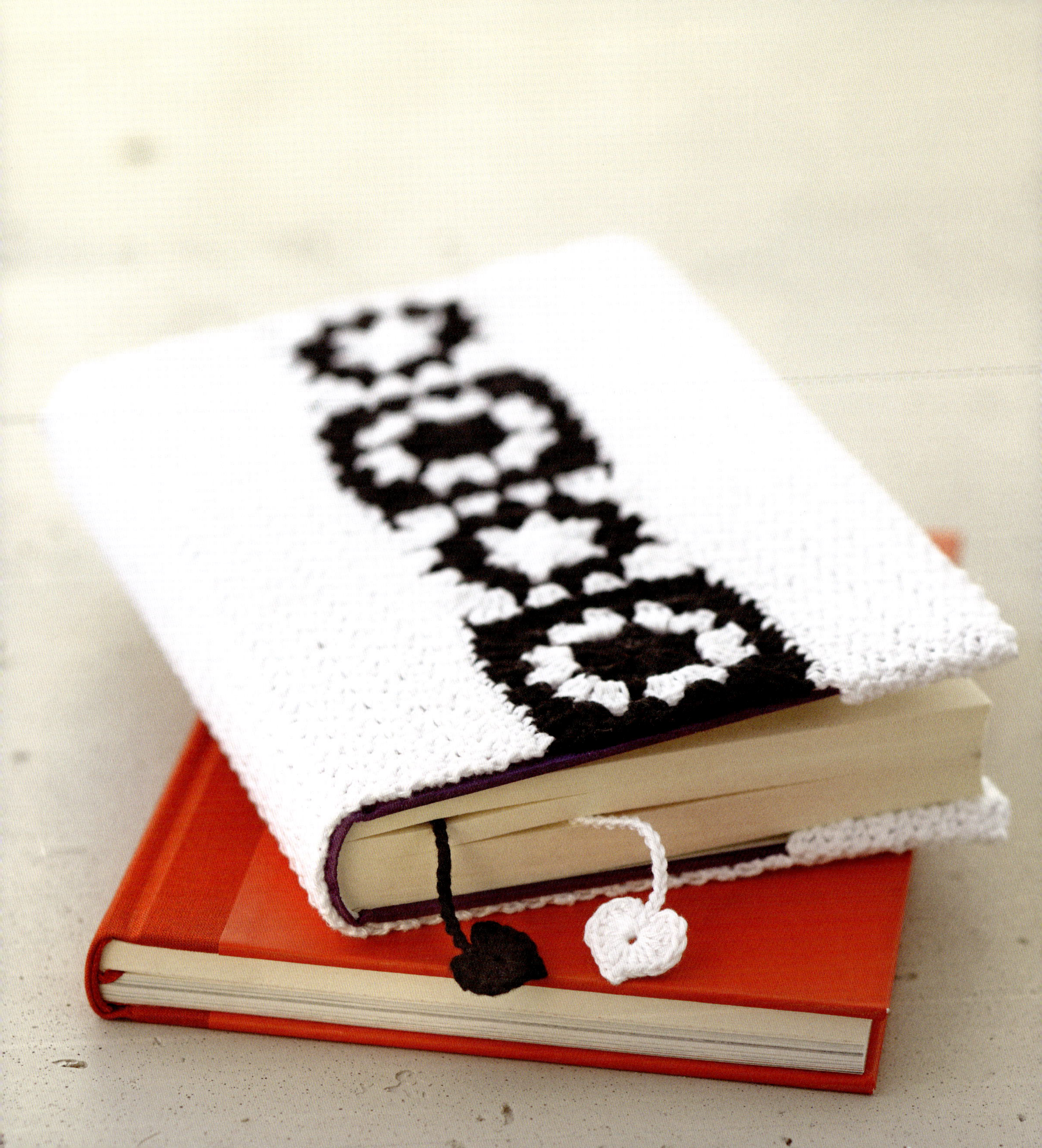

BLACK-AND-WHITE STORIES

BOOK COVER WITH BOOKMARKS

SKILL LEVEL

Experienced

FINISHED MEASUREMENTS:

Width 6¼ in / 16 cm, length 9 in / 23 cm

MATERIALS

Yarn: CYCA #3 (DK/light worsted), Schachenmayr Catania or equivalent (100% cotton; 137 yd/125 m / 50 g)

Yarn Amounts:
White #106, 150 g
Black #110, 50 g

Hook: U.S. size B-1 / 2.5 mm

Notions: Tapestry needle

Gauge: 26 sts and 19 rows = 4 x 4 in / 10 x 10 cm in Texture Stitch. Adjust needle size to obtain correct gauge if necessary.

Chart: Page 100

TEXTURE STITCH

Worked in rows.

Row 1: Ch 1 (turning ch), sc in first st, (dc in next st, sc in next st) to last st, dc in last st.

Rep Row 1 for patt.

INSTRUCTIONS

GRANNY SQUARES

With Black, make a magic ring.

Rnd 1 (Black): Ch 4, tr2tog (first cluster-st), ch 3, *tr3tog (second cluster-st), ch 3; rep from * 4 more times (6 cluster-sts). Join with sl st in 4th ch. Work another sl st in the next tr and another in 1st ch sp of Rnd 1 (between the cluster sts).

Rnd 2 (White): In 1st ch sp, work [ch 3, 2 dc, ch 3, 3 dc, ch 1], * in the next ch sp work [3 dc, ch 1, 3 dc, ch 1]; rep from * 4 more times. Join with sl st in the 3rd ch. Work another sl st in the next dc and another sl st in the ch of the prev rnd.

Rnd 3 (Black): In the first ch of the prev rnd work [ch 4, 2 tr, ch 3, 3 tr] (corner). Work 3 dc in each of the next 2 ch, *in the next ch work [3 tr, ch 3, 3 tr] (corner), work 3 dc in each of the next 2 ch; rep from * 2 more times. Join with sl st in 4th ch.

Make 3 more Granny Squares, working Rnds 1 and 2 as above and reversing colors on 2 of the squares (see photo). On Rnd 3, join the squares together as follows: In each ch sp at the corners and between each dc, join the squares together with a sl st. Weave in ends.

BOOK COVER

With the 4 attached Granny Squares held lengthwise, join White to the top right corner of the strip by pulling the tail through the ch sp and tying a knot. Ch 1, 2 sc in the ch sp, * 2 sc in the next 2 tr of the Granny Square, sc between the next 2 dc clusters; rep from * 3 more times, dc in last ch sp—15 sts in 1 Granny Square.

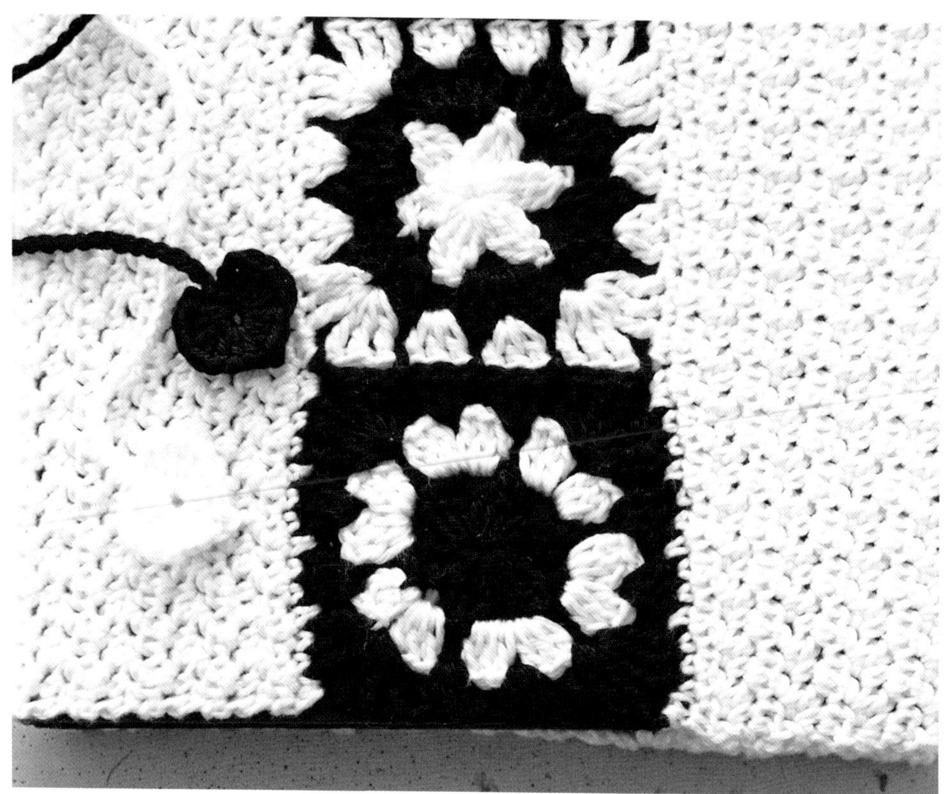

Work 15 sts in each Granny Square as above (60 sts total). Turn. Work in Texture Stitch. For the sort side, work 16 rows—3½ in / 9 cm. Fasten off and join yarn on other side of Granny Squares. For the long side, work in Pattern Stitch for 48 rows—10 in / 26 cm.

Tip: Adjust the length of the sides to fit the size of your book.

FINISHING

Weave in ends.

Fold approx. 3 in / 8 cm on each end to the WS and crochet in place.

HEART BOOKMARKS

With White, make a magic ring.

Rnd 1: (Ch 3, 4 dc, 3 hdc, ch 2, 3 hdc, 4 dc, ch 3, sl st) in the magic loop. Pull the tail to close the loop. Make a chain about 12 in / 30 cm long and sl st to the center of the top of the book cover.

Make a second bookmark with Black.

MODERN TOUCH

A STYLISH HOOD

SKILL LEVEL

Intermediate

FINISHED MEASUREMENTS:

Length 19½ in / 50 cm, hood width 9½ in / 24 cm, scarf legnth 67 in / 170 cm

MATERIALS

Yarn: CYCA #6 (super bulky/roving) Schachenmayr Merino Super Big Mix (50% merino, 50% acrylic; 87 yd/80 m / 100g)

Yarn Amounts:
White #99, 400 g
Black #101, 300 g

Hook: U.S. size L-11 / 8 mm

Notions: Tapestry needle, 4 buttons 1½ in / 4 cm in diameter, sewing needle and matching thread

Gauge: 10 sts and 7 rows = 4 x 4 in / 10 x 10 cm in V-Stitch. Adjust needle size to obtain correct gauge if necessary.

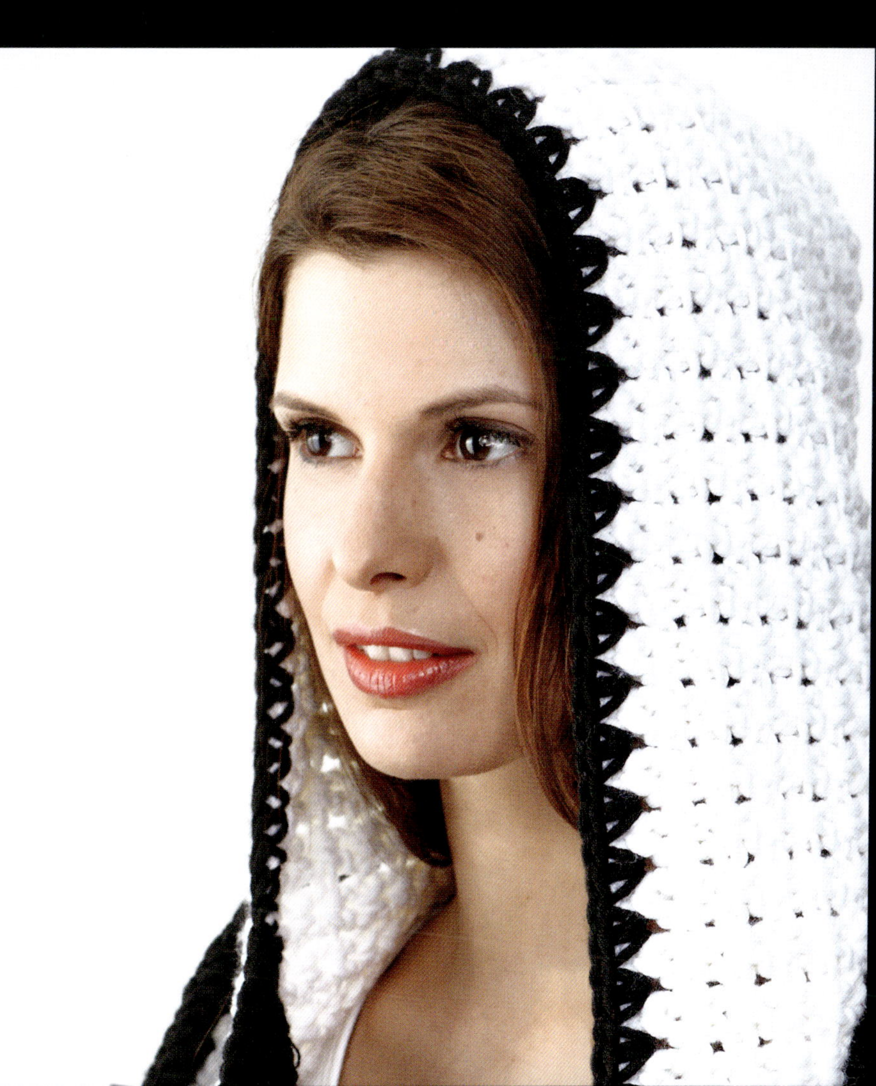

V-STITCH

Row 1: Ch 3 (turning ch), dc in first st, *sk 1 st, 2 dc in next st (V-st-group); rep from * across. End row with 2 dc in last st.

Row 2: Sl st in 2nd dc, sl st in the middle of the next V-st-group, ch 3 and dc in middle of next V-st-group, * 2 dc in middle of next V-st-group; rep from * across. End with 2 dc in middle of last V-st-group.

Rep Row 2 for patt.

INSTRUCTIONS

HOOD

With White, ch 89.

Row 1: Sc in second ch from hk and in each ch across—88 sc.

Rows 2–13: Work in V-Stitch.

The pattern offset is achieved by omitting the first and last V in every other row.

Row 14: Pm in center of row. Work as for Row 3, but for a pretty accent, dec in V-sts before and after marker—2 sts decreased.

Row 15: Rep Row 14.

Fold the hood in half with WS together and close the back seam.

SCARF

Join Black to the lower right corner of the hood.

Row 1: Ch 3 (turning ch), dc in first st, *sk 1 st, 2 dc in next st; rep from * 10 more times (12 V-st-groups).

Row 2: Sl st, ch 3, sc in middle of next V-st-group, *2 dc in middle of next V-st-group across.

Rows 3–6: Ch 3 (turning ch), dc in middle of first V-st-group, *2 dc in middle of next V-st group across.

Row 7: Rep Row 3. In the last dc-group, make 1 dc (decrease).

Row 8: Ch 3 (turning ch), dc in the middle of the next V-st-group, * 2 dc in the middle of the next V-st-group; rep from * across.

Row 9: Rep Row 3, including decrease at end of row.

Rows 10–12: Repeat Row 8, Row 9, and Row 8 once more.

Row 13: Repeat Row 3, but skip the last dc (11 V-st-groups).

Rows 14–101: Repeat Rows 7–13, continuing to decrease.

Row 102: For the buttonhole, ch 1, sc in each of the first 3 dc, ch 4, sk 2 dc, sc in each of the next 3 dc.

Sc around the shawl. Across the front of the hood, sc in the middle of each V-st-group. On the back of the shawl, end with dc. Work 4 sc in the 4-ch buttonhole.

FINISHING

Weave in ends. Sew button on to the left side at the lower-left corner.

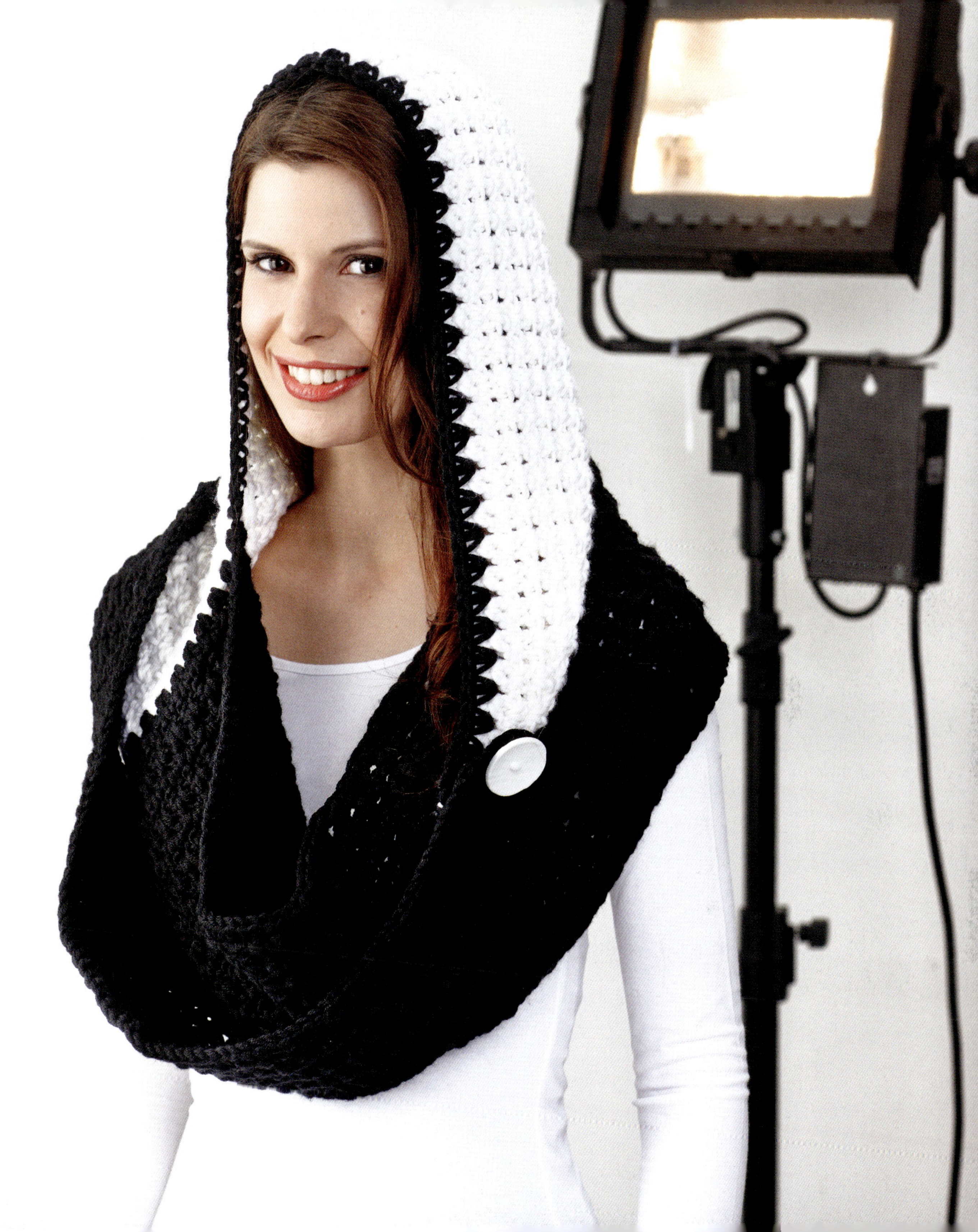

ZIGZAG LUCK

DRAWSTRING BAG WITH STRIPES

SKILL LEVEL

Experienced

FINISHED MEASUREMENTS:

Length 15¾ in / 40 cm, diameter 11½ in / 29 cm

MATERIALS

Yarn: CYCA #5 (chunky/craft/rug) Schachenmayr Bravo Mezzo or equivalent (100% acrylic; 180 yd/165 / 100 g)

Yarn Amounts:
Black #99, 300 g
White #01, 100 g

Hook: U.S. size H-8 / 5 mm

Notions: Tapestry needle

Gauge: 21 sts and 14 rows = 4 x 4 in / 10 x 10 cm in Zigzag Stitch. Adjust needle size to obtain correct gauge if necessary.

ZIGZAG STITCH

Row 1: 2 sc in the 2nd ch from hk, *6 sc, insert hk into next ch and draw up a lp, sk next 2 ch, insert hk into next ch and draw up a lp, yo hk and draw yarn through all 3 lps, 6 sc, 3 sc in next ch; rep from * 2 more times, 6 sc, insert hk into next ch and draw up a lp, sk next 2 ch, insert hk into next ch and draw up a lp, yo hk and draw yarn through all 3 lps, 6 sc, 2 sc in last ch.

Row 2: Ch 1 (turning ch), 2 sc in first st, *6 sc, insert hk into next st and draw up a lp, sk next st, insert hk into next st and draw up a lp, yo hk and draw yarn through all 3 lps, 6 sc, 3 sc in next st; rep from * 2 more times, 6 sc, insert hk into next st and draw up a lp, sk next st, insert hk into next st and draw up a lp, yo hk and draw yarn through all 3 lps, 2 sc in last st.

Rep Row 2 for patt.

BORDER PATTERN

The border at the top of the bag is worked in rounds with sc, then with dc, and elongated sc. To work elongated sc, do not insert the hk in to the next st on the previous row, but under the stitch 2 rows below (see page 106), which explains elongated double crochet.

INSTRUCTIONS

BOTTOM

Worked in the round, beginning with 1 turning ch and ending with a sl st to join.

With Black, make a magic ring.

Rnd 1: Ch 1 and 9 sc in magic ring, join with sl st (9 sts).

Rnd 2: 2 sc in each sc around (18 sts).

Rnd 3: (Sc in each of the next 2 sc, 2 sc in next sc) around (24 sts).

Rnd 4: (Sc in each of the next 3 sc, 2 sc in next sc) around (30 sts).

Rnd 5: (Sc in each of the next 4 sc, 2 sc in next sc) around (36 sts).

Rnd 6: (Sc in each of the next 5 sc, 2 sc in next sc) around (42 sts).

Rnds 7–20: Continue increasing 6 sts in each rnd as above (126 sts).

Piece should measure approx. 11½ in / 29 cm.

Cut yarn.

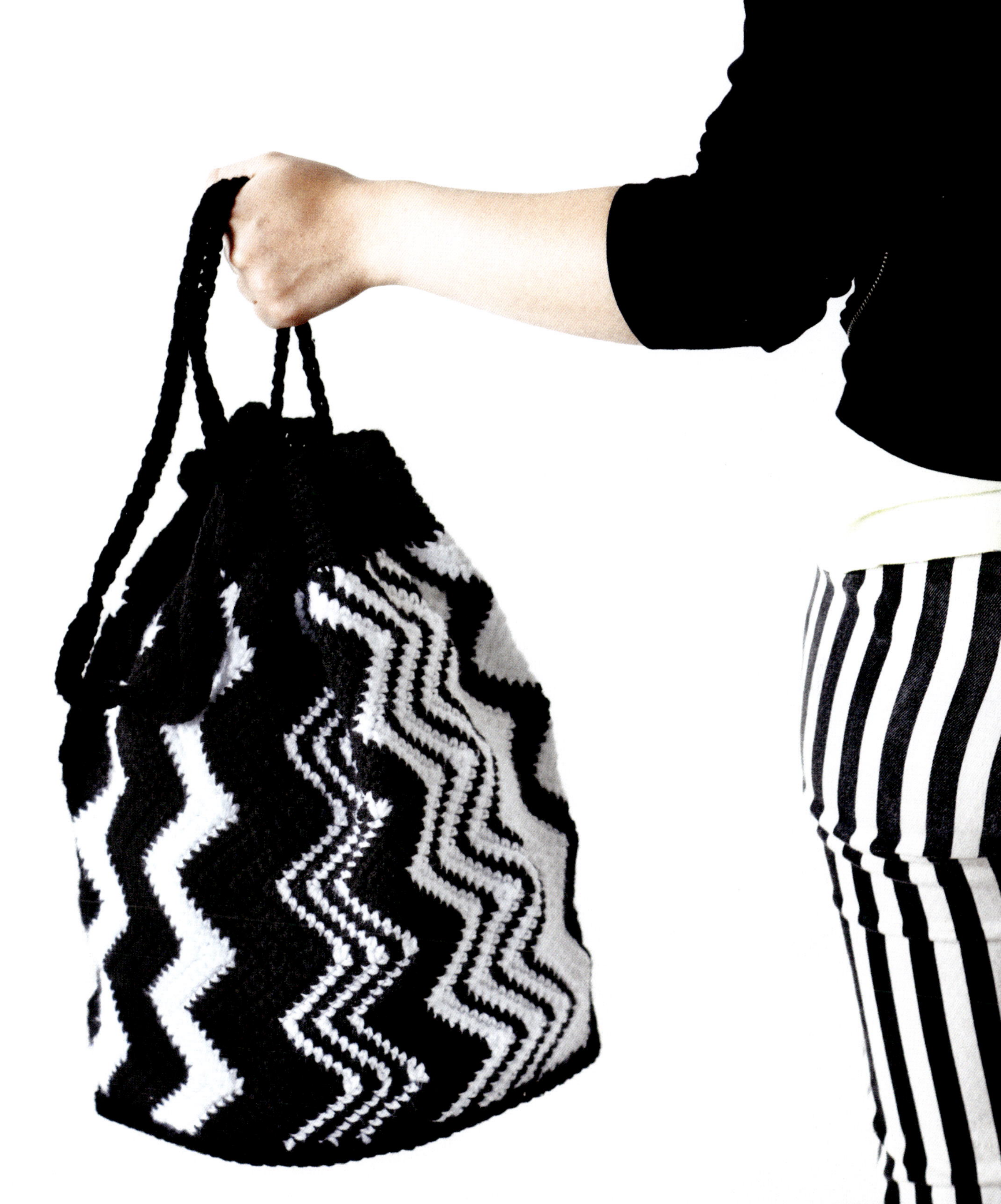

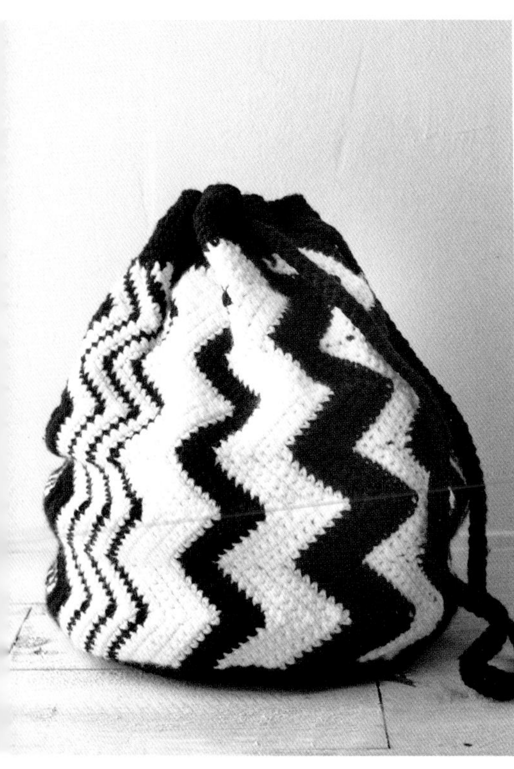

BAG SIDES

Ch 20 and work in rows.

Rows 1 and 2: Work in Zigzag Stitch (65 sts).

Rep Row 2, changing colors as desired for stripe pattern, until piece measures approx. 36 in / 91 cm. The length of the bag sides must equal the circumference of the bag bottom.

With RS together, use sc to close side seam. Turn right side out so seam is on the inside.

TOP BAND

Join Black to the bag sides at the seam and work in the round.

Rnd 1: Ch 1, sc in each edge stitch around, join with sl st.

Rnds 2–4: Ch 1, sc in each sc around, join with sl st.

Rnd 5: Ch 3, dc in each sc around, join with sl st to 3rd ch.

Rnd 6: Ch 1, work 1 elongated sc in each dc around, join with sl st.

Rnds 7–9: Ch 1, sc in each st around, join with sl st.

CORD

With Black, make a chain approx. 36 in / 90 cm long. Sc in 2nd ch from hk and in each ch across to last ch, 3 sc in last ch. Turn and on the opposite side of the foundation chain, sc in each ch across to last ch, 2 sc in last ch (with the first sc made, there will now be 3 sc in this ch). Sl st in first sc. Cut yarn.

FINISHING

Lay the bag sides on a flat surface and use string to mark the bottom 2 corners. Fold the bag in half so it is divided into 4 equal sections and mark the 2 additional corners. Fold the bottom in half and mark the two edges at the fold line, then fold it again into quarters and mark the additional fold points. Line up the markers on the bag sides with the markers on the bottom and use single crochet to join the pieces.

Weave the cord through the top edge, going in an out of the crochet about 5 or 6 stitches apart, starting and ending on the outside of the bag. Sew the ends of the cord together. Weave in ends.

CONCEALED IN BLACK AND WHITE

HANDY PHONE AND TABLET CASES

SKILL LEVEL

Easy

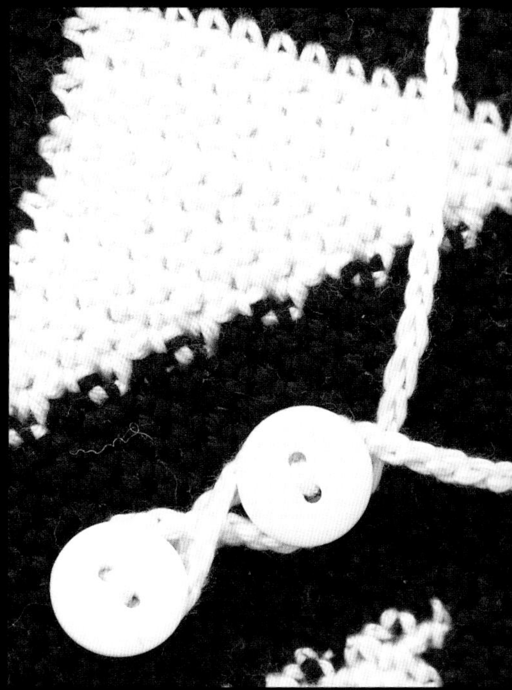

PHONE CASE

FINISHED MEASUREMENTS:

Length 6 in / 15 cm, width 3¾ in / 8.5 cm

MATERIALS

Yarn: CYCA #3 (DK/light worsted), Schachenmayr Catania or equivalent (100% cotton; 137 yd/125 m / 50 g)

Yarn Amounts:
White #106, 50 g
Black #110, 50 g

Hook: U.S. size C-2 or D-3 / 3 mm

Notions: Tapestry needle, 2 white buttons ¾ in / 2 cm in diameter, sewing needle and matching thread

Gauge: 19 sc and 19 rows = 4 x 4 in / 10 x 10 cm. Adjust needle size to obtain correct gauge if necessary.

TABLET CASE

FINISHED MEASUREMENTS:

Length 7 in / 18 cm, width 11 in / 28 cm

MATERIALS

Yarn: CYCA #4 (worsted/afghan/aran), Schachenmayr Catania Grande or equivalent (100% cotton; 68 yd/62 m / 50 g)

Yarn Amounts:
White #3106, 150 g
Black #3110, 50 g

Hook: U.S. size G-6 / 4 mm

Notions: Tapestry needle, 2 black buttons ¾ in / 2 cm in diameter, sewing needle and matching thread

Gauge: 18 sc and 18 rows = 4 x 4 in / 10 x 10 cm. Adjust needle size to obtain correct gauge if necessary.

Chart: Page 97

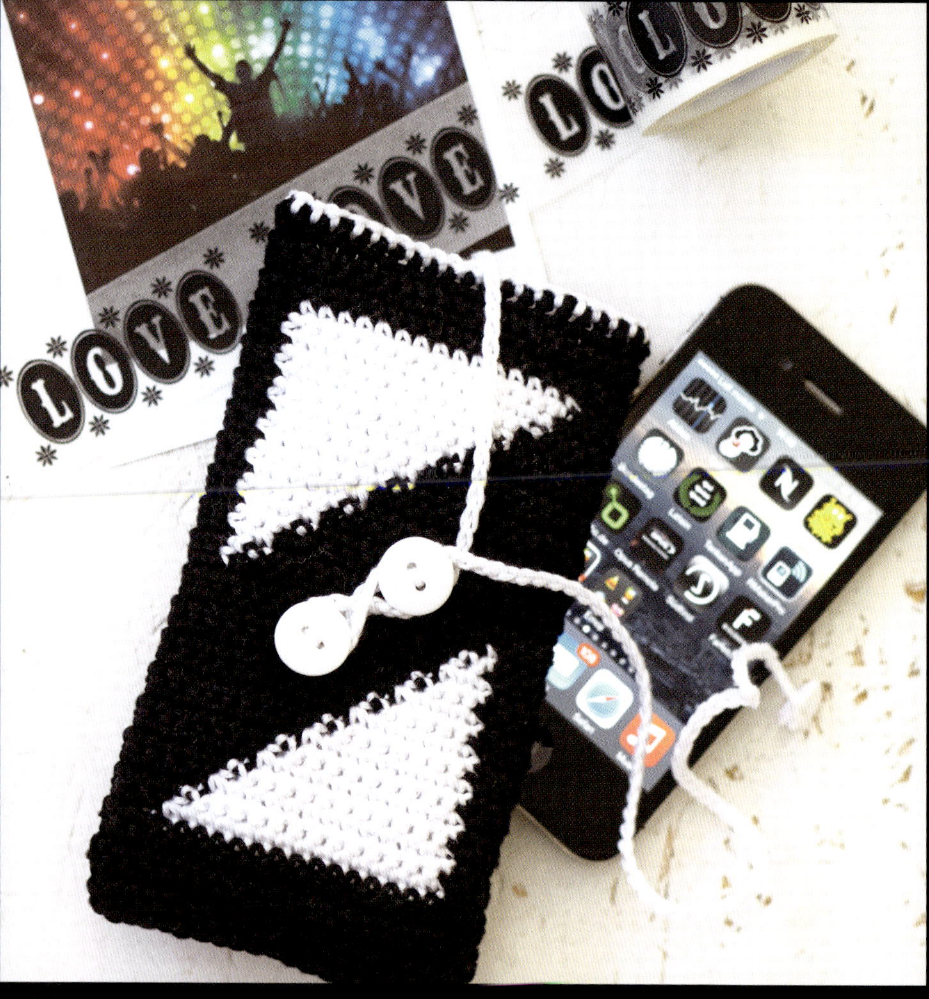

PHONE CASE

With Black, ch 42 and join with sl st to form a ring.

Rnd 1 (Black): Ch 1, sc in each ch around, join with sl st (42 sts).

Rnds 2–6 (Black): Ch 1, sc in each sc around, join with sl st (42 sts).

Rnds 7–37: With Black, ch 1, 3 sc; work chart over next 15 sts; with Black, work 24 sc.

Rnds 38–43 (Black): Ch 1, sc in each sc around, join with sl st (42 sts).

FINISHING

Weave in ends.

Sew buttons to front of case between the triangles. Make a 12 in / 30 cm chain and work a 4-dc bobble in the last st. Attach the chain to the center back of the case.

TABLET CASE

With White, ch 33 and work back and forth in rows.

Row 1 (White): Sc in 2nd ch from hk and each sc around (32 sts).

Rows 2–5 (White): Ch 1 (turning ch), sc in each sc around.

Rows 6–49: With White, ch 1, 5 sc; work chart over next 22 sts; with White, 5 sc.

Rows 50–110 (White): Ch 1, sc in each sc around.

FINISHING

With RS facing out, fold the case in half and join pieces with sc along the short side and the long side. Weave in ends.

Sew buttons to front of case between the triangles. Make a 12 in / 30 cm chain and work a 4-dc bobble in the last st. Attach the chain to the center back of the case.

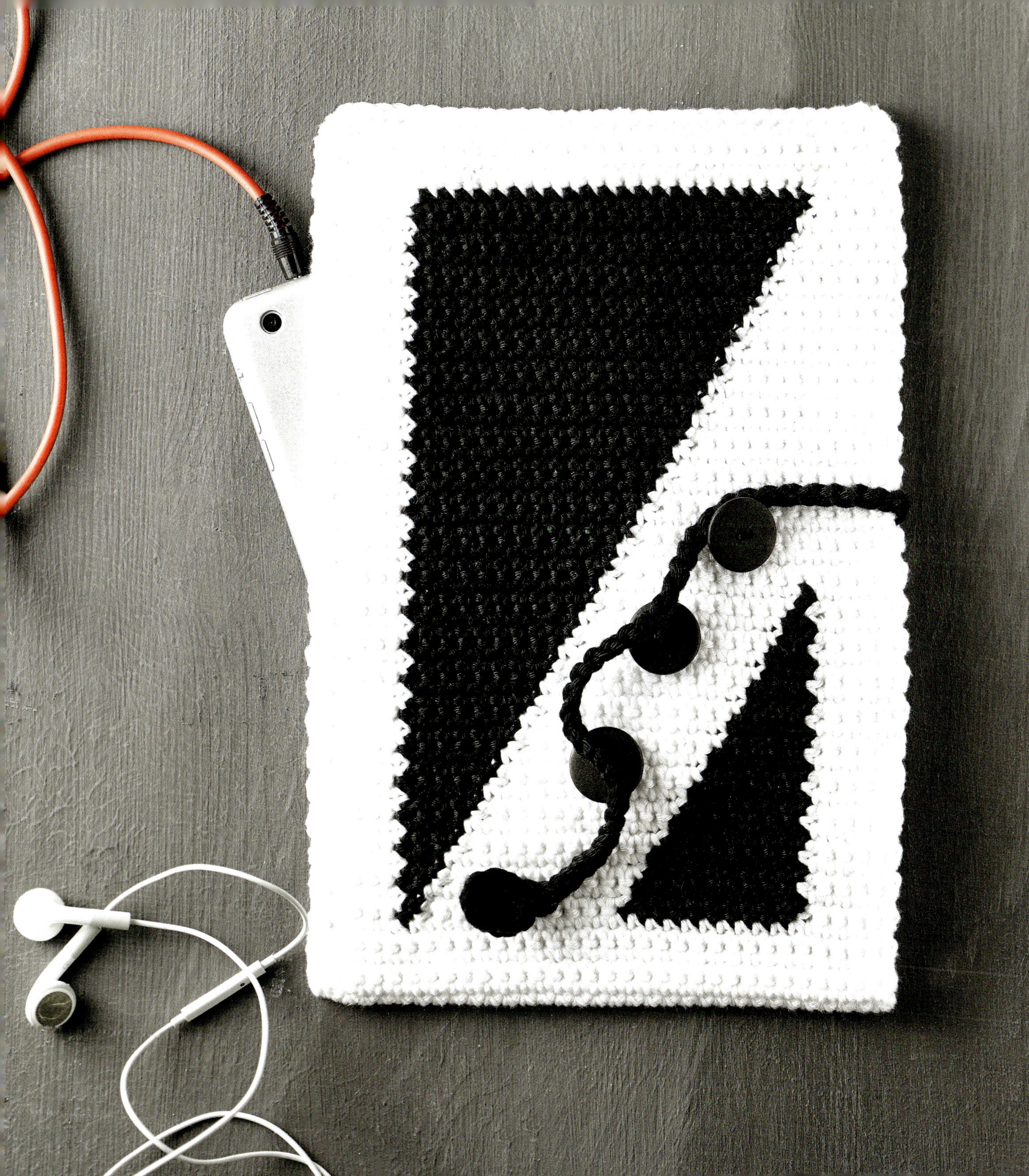

CUDDLY FRIENDS

STRIPED MITTENS

RIBBING

Ribbing is worked in rows with sc worked through the back loop only. Each row begins with 1 turning ch.

STRIPE PATTERN

Rnd 1 (Black): Ch 1, sc in each sc across, join with sl st.
Rnd 2 (White): Ch 2, hc in each sc across, join with sl st.
Rep Rows 1 and 2 for patt.

INSTRUCTIONS

Mittens are worked with 2 strands of yarn held together.
With Black, ch 10.
Row 1: Sc in 2nd sc from hk and in each ch across (9 sts).
Rows 2–21: Work in Ribbing (9 sts).
Do not cut yarn. Begin working in the round as follows:
Rnd 1 (Black): Ch 1, sc into the sts on the side edge of Ribbing and inc 3 sts evenly spaced (28 sc).
Rnds 2–11: Work in Stripe Pattern (28 sts).

LEFT THUMB OPENING

Rnd 12 (Black): Ch 4, sk 7 sts, sl st to the 8th st, sc in each st to end of rnd, join with sl st in first ch.
Rnd 13 (White): Ch 2, work 1 hdc in 4-ch sp, 21 hdc, join with sl st (25 sts).

RIGHT THUMB OPENING

Rnd 12 (Black): Ch 1, 21 sc, ch 4, sk the last 7 sts, join with sl st.
Rnd 13 (White): Ch 2, 21 hdc, work 1 hdc in the 4-ch sp, join with sl st (25 sts).

RIGHT AND LEFT HANDS

Rnds 14–19: Work in Stripe Pattern (25 sts).
Rnd 23 (Black): (3 sc, sc2tog) around (20 sc).
Rnd 24 (Black): Ch 1, sc in each sc around, join with sl st.
Rnd 25 (Black): (2 sc, sc2tog) around (15 sc).
Rnd 26 (Black): Ch 1, sc in each sc around, join with sl st.
Rnd 27 (Black): (Sc, sc2tog) around (10 sc).
Rnd 28 (Black): Ch 1, sc in each sc around, join with sl st.
Cut yarn, leaving an 8 in / 20 cm tail.

THUMB

Join Black to any stitch at the thumb opening.
Rnd 1: Ch 1, sc around—working 7 sc across the bottom of the thumb opening and 4 across the top/back—and join with sl st (11 sts).
Rnds 2–8: Ch 1, sc in each sc around, join with sl st.
Rnd 9: Ch 1, sc in next st, (sc2tog) across, join with sl st (6 sts).
Cut yarn, leaving a tail 6 in / 15 cm long.

FINISHING

Use the tails to gather in the tops of the hand and thumb. Sew the side seam on the cuff. Weave in ends.

SKILL LEVEL

Experienced

FINISHED MEASUREMENTS:

Total length 11 in / 27.5 cm, ribbing length 2½ in / 6.5 cm, width without thumbs 4½ in / 11.5 cm

MATERIALS

Yarn: CYCA #4 (worsted/afghan/aran), Schachenmayr Micro Grande or equivalent (100% acrylic; 218 yd/199 m / 100 g)

Yarn Amounts:
Black #199, 200 g
White #101, 100 g

Hook: U.S. size J-10 / 6 mm

Notions: Tapestry needle

Gauge: 13 sts and 12 rows = 4 x 4 in / 10 x 10 cm in Stripe Pattern. Adjust needle size to obtain correct gauge if necessary.

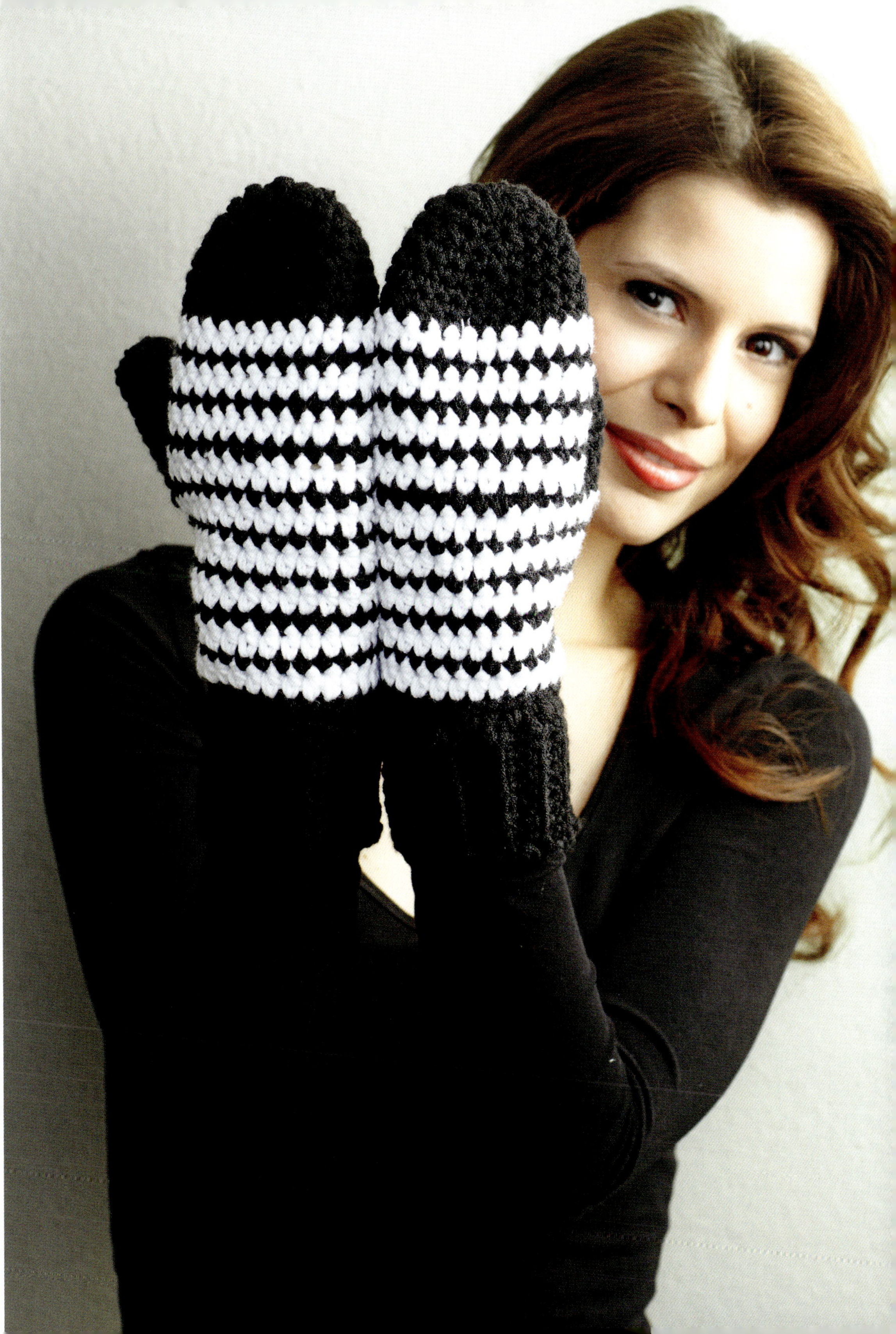

MAKING WAVES

COOL MESH BAG

SKILL LEVEL

Intermediate

FINISHED MEASUREMENTS:

15½ x 15½ in / 39 x 39 cm

MATERIALS

Yarn: CYCA #4 (worsted/afghan/aran), Schachenmayr Catania Grande or equivalent (100% cotton; 68 yd/62 m / 50 g)

Yarn Amounts:
Black #3110, 250 g
White #3106, 150 g

Hook: U.S. size G-6 / 4 mm

Notions: Tapestry needle

Gauge: 18 sc and 18 rows = 4 x 4 in / 10 x 10 cm. Adjust needle size to obtain correct gauge if necessary.

Chart(s): Page 99

WAVE PATTERN

Rnd 1 (Black): Work Chart A (120 sts).

Rnds 2 and 3 (White): Work Chart B (120 sts).

Rnds 4 and 5 (Black): Work Chart A (120 sts).

Rnds 6–29: Rep Rnds 2–5 another 6 times.

Rnds 30 and 31 (White): Work Chart B (120 sts).

Rnd 32 (Black): Work Chart A (120 sts).

INSTRUCTIONS

BOTTOM

With Black, ch 56.

Row 1: Sc in 2nd ch from hk and in each ch across (55 sts).

Rows 2–7: Ch 1 (turning ch), sc in each sc across (55 sts).

Do not cut yarn.

SIDES

Begin working in rounds.

Rnd 1: Ch 1; working around all sides of bottom piece, sc around, working 1 sc in each corner, and then join with sl st (120 sts).

Rnds 2–14: Ch 1, sc in each sc around, join with sl st.

Rnds 15–47: Work in Wave Pattern.

TOP

Rnds 47–49: Ch 1, sc in each sc around, join with sl st (120 sts).

Rnd 50: Ch 1, sc in each of next 29 sc, ch 20, sk 20 sts, sc in each of next 40 sts, ch 20, sk 20 sts, sc in next 11 sts, join with sl st.

Rnd 51: Ch 1, sc around—working into each sc and ch (not into the ch sp)—and join with sl st (120 sts).

Rnds 52–55: Ch 1, sc in each sc around, join with sl st.

FINISHING

Weave in ends.

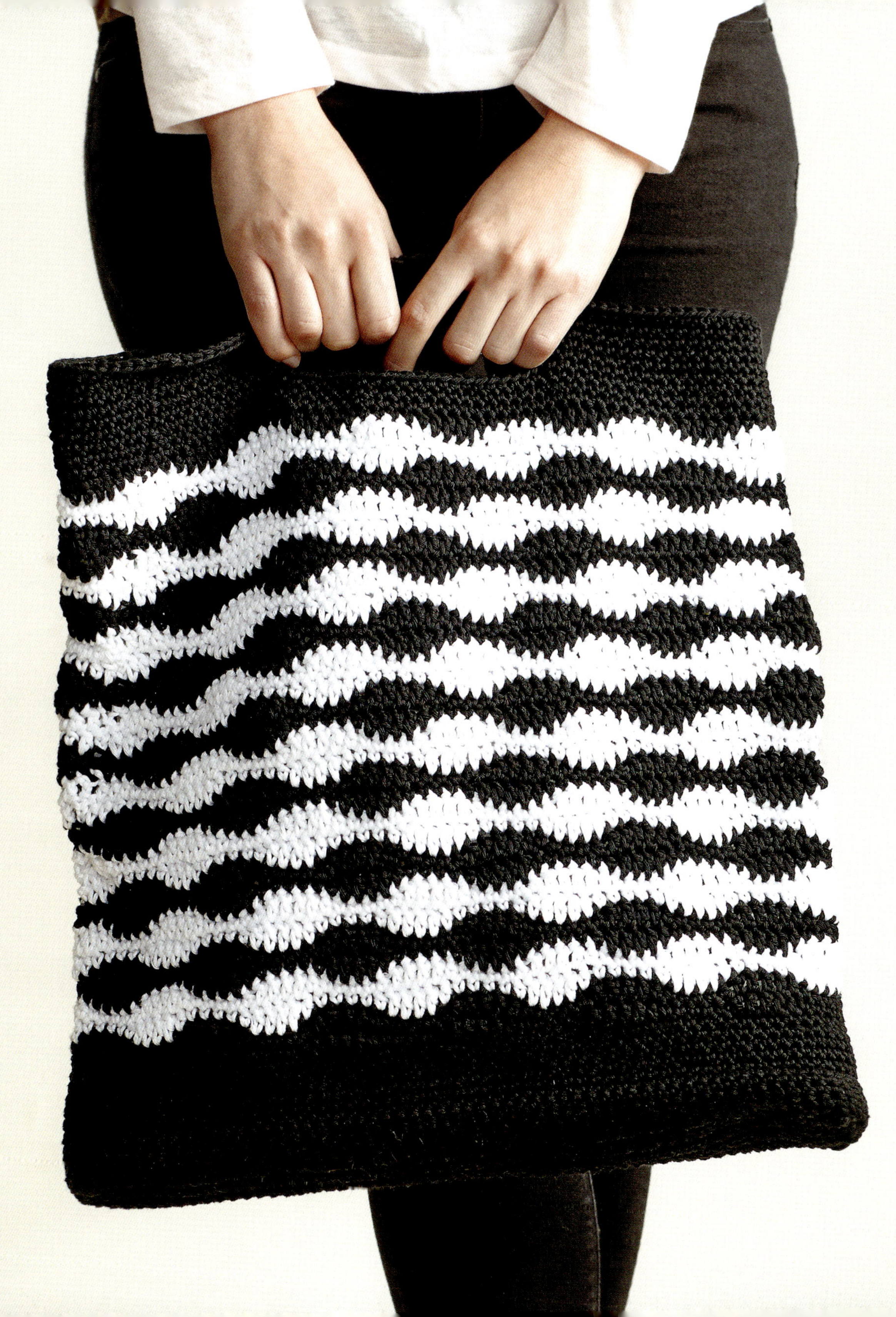

DANCE IN CIRCLES

WARM SLIPPER SOCKS

SKILL LEVEL

Intermediate

FINISHED MEASUREMENTS:

To fit women's U.S. shoe sizes 6½ to 9 / European sizes 37–40

MATERIALS

Yarn: CYCA #6 (super bulky/roving) Schachenmayr Merino Super Big Mix (50% merino, 50% acrylic; 87 yd/80 m / 100g)

Yarn Amounts:
Black #99, 200 g
White #01, 100 g

Hook: U.S. size L-11 / 8 mm

Notions: Tapestry needle

Gauge: 10 dc and 7 rows = 4 x 4 in / 10 x 10 cm. Adjust needle size to obtain correct gauge if necessary.

V-STITCH

Rnd 1: Ch 2 (counts as 1 hdc), hdc in next st, sk next st, * 2 hdc in next st, sk next st; rep from * around, join with sl st in first hdc.

INSTRUCTIONS

With Black, make a magic ring.

Rnd 1 (Black): Ch 3, 11 dc in ring (12 sts).

Rnd 2 (White): Ch 2, (hdc in next 5 sts, 2 hdc in next st) twice, join with sl st (24 sts).

Rnd 3: (Black): Ch 3, dc in back loop around, join with sl st.

Rnd 4 (White): Work in V-stitch.

Rnds 5–13: Rep Rnds 3 and 4.

HEEL

With Black, work in rows.

Rows 1–6: Ch 1, sc 18, turn.

Row 7: Ch 1, sc in next 8 sc, sc2tog, sc in next 8 sc (17 sts).

Row 8: Ch 1, sc in next 7 sc, sc3tog, sc in next 7 sc (15 sts).

Row 9: Ch 1, sc in next 6 sc, sc3tog, sc in next 6 sc (13 sts).

Cut the yarn. Fold the heel in half with RS facing out and use the tail to sew the 6 sts together.

LEG

Join White and return to working in the round, continuing from Rnd 13 and beginning at the center of the heel.

Rnd 14 (White): Ch 2, 1 hdc. Along first side of heel, work (2 hdc in same st) 4 times, skipping sts in between to distribute evenly along side of heel. Across front of ankle, work (3 hdc in same st) once, (2 hdc in same st) twice, and (3 hdc in same st) once, again skipping sts in between to distribute evenly across front of ankle. Work second side of heel as for first side of heel, and join at back center of heel with sl st (28 sts).

Rnd 15 (Black): Ch 3, dc in back loop around, join with sl st (28 sts).

Rnds 16–25: Change colors and work in V-st, repeating Rnds 3 and 4.

FINISHING

Work (ch 1, sl st) around top edge.

Weave in ends.

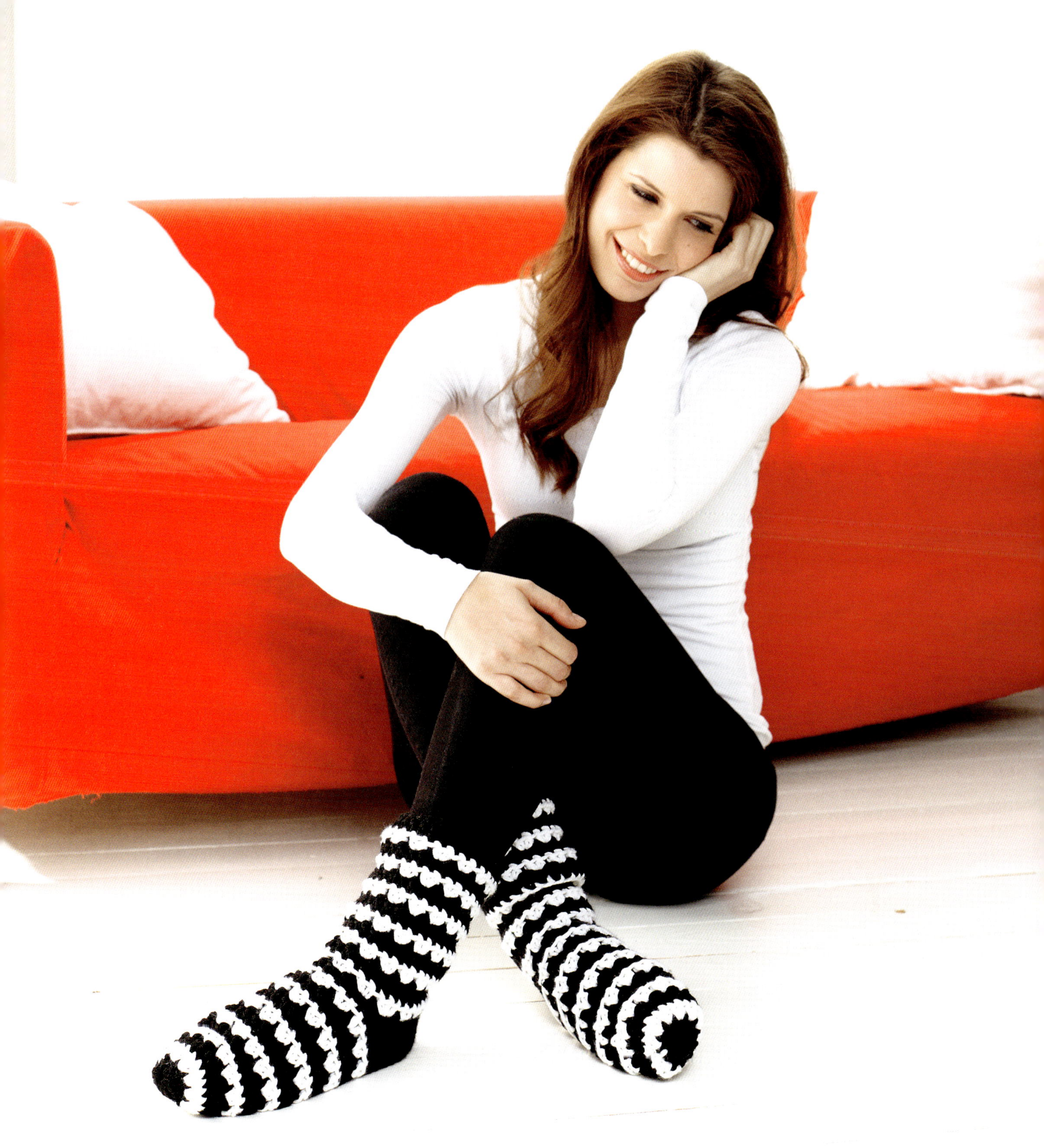

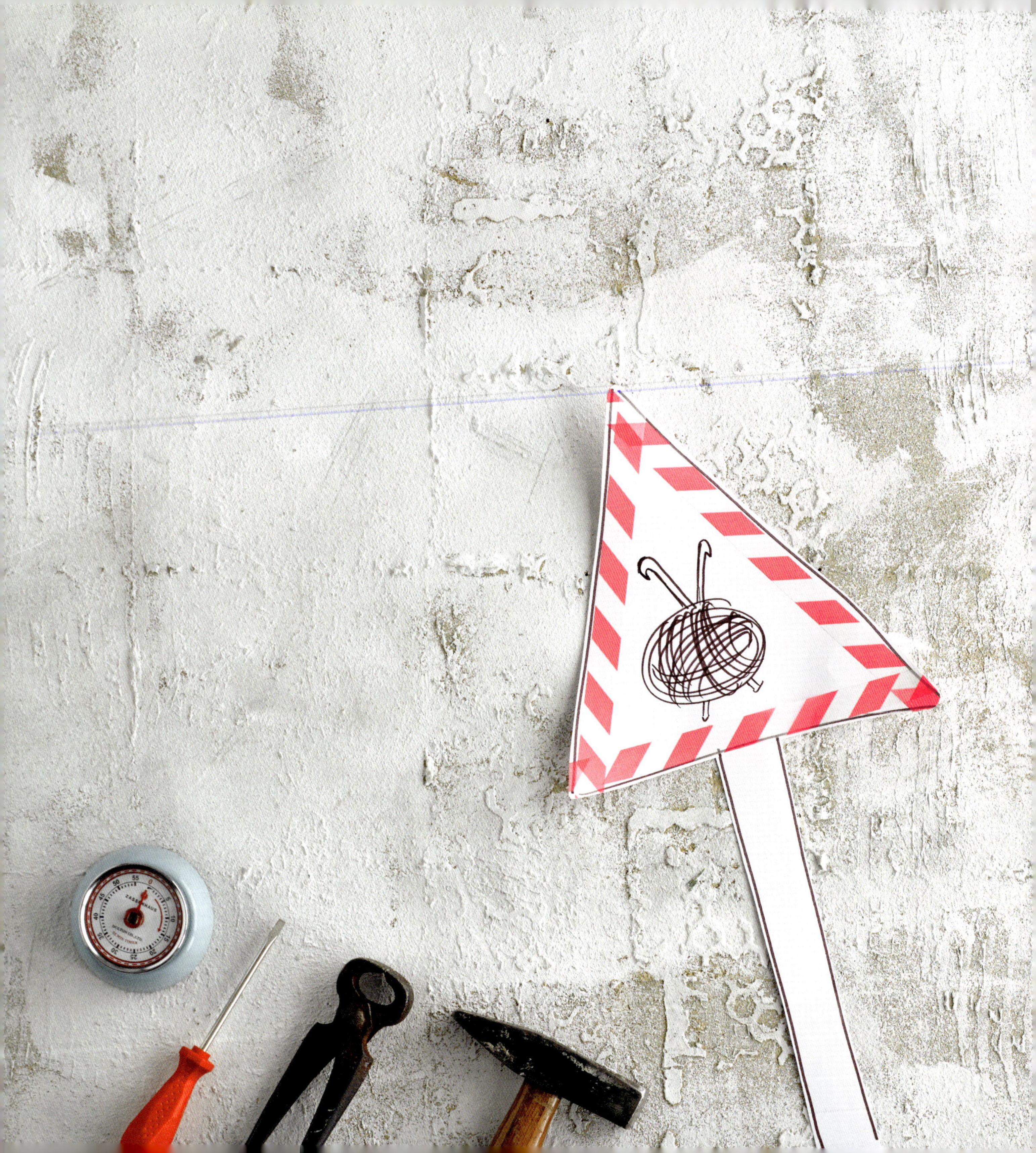

HOME WORK

Rnd 1: Ch 1, work 10 hdc in magic ring (11 sts). Pull the loop on the hook to enlarge it and set it aside to be worked later. Place marker in first dc. Join White and ch 1. Pull Black tail to close magic loop. Sl st in each Black hdc around. Pull the loop on the hook to enlarge it and set it aside to be worked later.

Rnd 2: Insert hk into Black loop. Work 2 hdc in each st, always working into the previous Black dc and not into the White sl sts (22 sts). Move the marker up. Set Black loop aside. With White, sl st in each st around. Set White loop aside.

Continue to alternate between White and Black in this fashion, working the increases and decreases in the Black dc sections as follows:

Rnd 3: Work as for Rnd 2, increasing in every 2nd st (33 sts).

Rnd 4: Work as for Rnd 2, increasing in every 3rd st (44 sts).

6th st (77 sts).

Rnd 8: Work as for Rnd 2, increasing in every 7th st (88 sts).

Rnds 9 and 10: With Black, dc in each dc and with White, st st in each dc. Place marker on Rnd 10 (88 sts).

Rnd 11: (Dc in next 6 sts, dc2tog) around (77 sts).

Rnd 12: (Dc in next 5 sts, dc2tog) around (66 sts).

Rnd 13: (Dc in next 4 sts, dc2tog) around (55 sts).

Rnd 14: (Dc in next 3 sts, dc2tog) around (44 sts).

Rnd 15: Dc in each dc around (44 sts).

Insert the bag with the sand.

Rnd 16: (Dc in next 2 sts, dc2tog) around (33 sts).

Rnd 17: Dc in each dc around (33 sts).

Rnd 18: (Dc in next st, dc2tog) around (22 sts).

Rnds 19 and 20: Dc in each dc around (22 sts).

sts).

Cut yarn.

FINISHING

Use the tail to gather in the final 5 sts and close the top. Weave in ends.

SKILL LEVEL

Intermediate

FINISHED MEASUREMENTS:

Diameter 10½ in / 27 cm, height 19 in / 48 cm

MATERIALS

Yarn: CYCA #6 (super bulky/ roving) Schachenmayr Boston or equivalent (70% acrylic, 30% wool; 131 yd/120 m / 200 g)

Yarn Amounts:
Black #99, 150 g
White #101, 50 g

Hook: U.S. size K-10½ / 7 mm

Notions: Tapestry needle, 2 stitch markers, bag of matching dimensions filled with sand

Gauge: 13 dc and 5 rows = 4 x 4 in / 10 x 10 cm. Adjust needle size to obtain correct gauge if necessary.

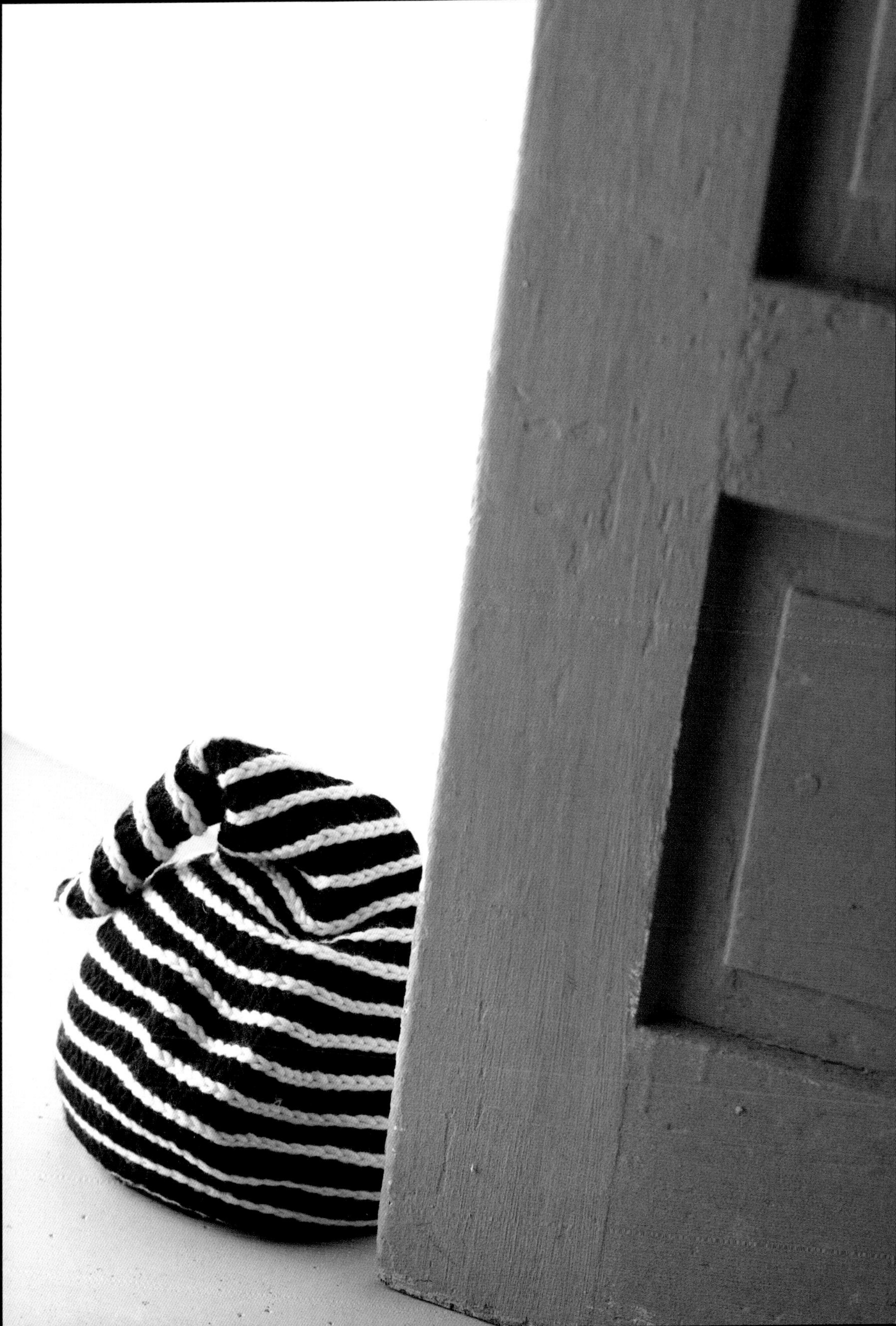

COOL STORAGE

BASKETS WITH PANACHE

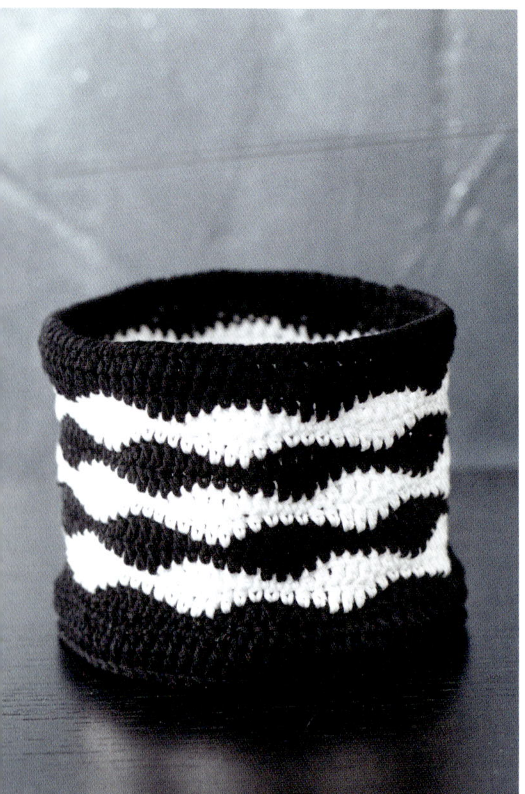

SKILL LEVEL

Intermediate

SMALL BASKET

FINISHED MEASUREMENTS:

Diameter approx. 4¾ in / 12 cm, height 5 in / 13 cm

MATERIALS

Yarn: CYCA #4 (worsted/afghan/aran), Schachenmayr Catania Grande or equivalent (100% cotton; 68 yd/62 m / 50 g)

Yarn Amounts:
White #3106, 100 g
Black #3110, 50 g

Hook: U.S. size G-6 / 4 mm

Notions: Tapestry needle

MEDIUM BASKET

FINISHED MEASUREMENTS:

Diameter approx. 6½ in / 17 cm, height 5 in / 13 cm

MATERIALS

Yarn: CYCA #4 (worsted/afghan/aran), Schachenmayr Catania Grande or equivalent (100% cotton; 68 yd/62 m / 50 g)

Yarn Amounts:
White #3106, 100 g
Black #3110, 50 g

Hook: U.S. size G-6 / 4 mm

Notions: Tapestry needle

LARGE BASKET

FINISHED MEASUREMENTS:

Diameter approx. 8½ in / 22 cm, height 5 in / 13 cm

MATERIALS

Yarn: CYCA #4 (worsted/afghan/aran), Schachenmayr Catania Grande or equivalent (100% cotton; 68 yd/62 m / 50 g)

Yarn Amounts:
White #3106, 150 g
Black #3110, 50 g

Hook: U.S. size G-6 / 4 mm

Notions: Tapestry needle

Gauge: 18 hdc and 18 rows = 4 x 4 in / 10 x 10 cm. Adjust needle size to obtain correct gauge if necessary.

Charts: Page 99

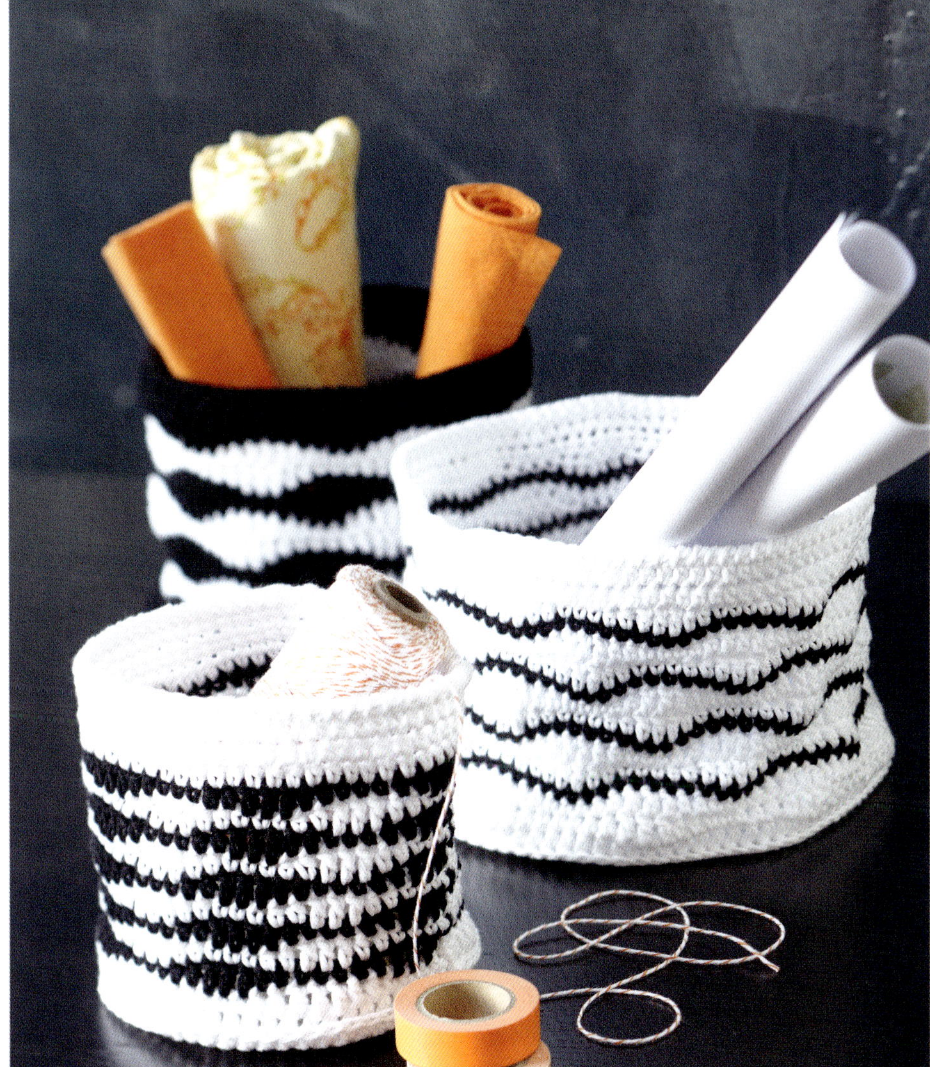

SMALL BASKET

With White, make a magic ring.

Rnd 1 (White): Ch 2 and work 7 hdc in magic ring, join with sl st (8 sts).

Rnd 2 (White): 2 hdc in each st around (16 sts).

Rnd 3 (White): (Hdc in next st, 2 hdc in next st) around (24 sts).

Rnd 4 (White): (Hdc in next 2 sts, 2 hdc in next st) around (32 sts).

Rnd 5 (White): (Hdc in next 3 sts, 2 hdc in next st) around (40 sts).

Rnd 6 (White): (Hdc in next 4 sts, 2 hdc in next st) around (48 sts).

Rnd 7 (White): (Hdc in next 5 sts, 2 hdc in next st) around (56 sts).

Rnd 8 (White): (Hdc in next 11 sts, 2 hdc in next st) 4 times, hdc in each st to end of rnd (60 sts).

Rnd 9 (White): Ch 1, hdc in each hdc around, join with sl st (60 sts).

Rnd 10 (White): Ch 2, hdc in back loops around, join with sl st.

Rnd 11 (White): Work as charted.

Rnd 12 (Black): Work as charted.

Rnds 13–20: Rep Rnds 11 and 12.

Rnds 21–23 (White): Ch 2, hdc in each st around, join with sl st.

MEDIUM BASKET

With Black, make a magic ring.

Rnd 1 (Black): Ch 2 and work 7 hdc in magic ring, join with sl st (8 sts).

Rnd 2 (Black): 2 hdc in each st around (16 sts).

Rnd 3 (Black): (Hdc in next st, 2 hdc in next st) around (24 sts).

Rnd 4 (Black): (Hdc in next 2 sts, 2 hdc in next st) around (32 sts).

Rnd 5 (Black): (Hdc in next 3 sts, 2 hdc in next st) around (40 sts).

Rnd 6 (Black): (Hdc in next 4 sts, 2 hdc in next st) around (48 sts).

Rnd 7 (Black): (Hdc in next 5 sts, 2 hdc in next st) around (56 sts).

Rnd 8 (Black): (Hdc in next 6 sts, 2 hdc in next st) around (64 sts).

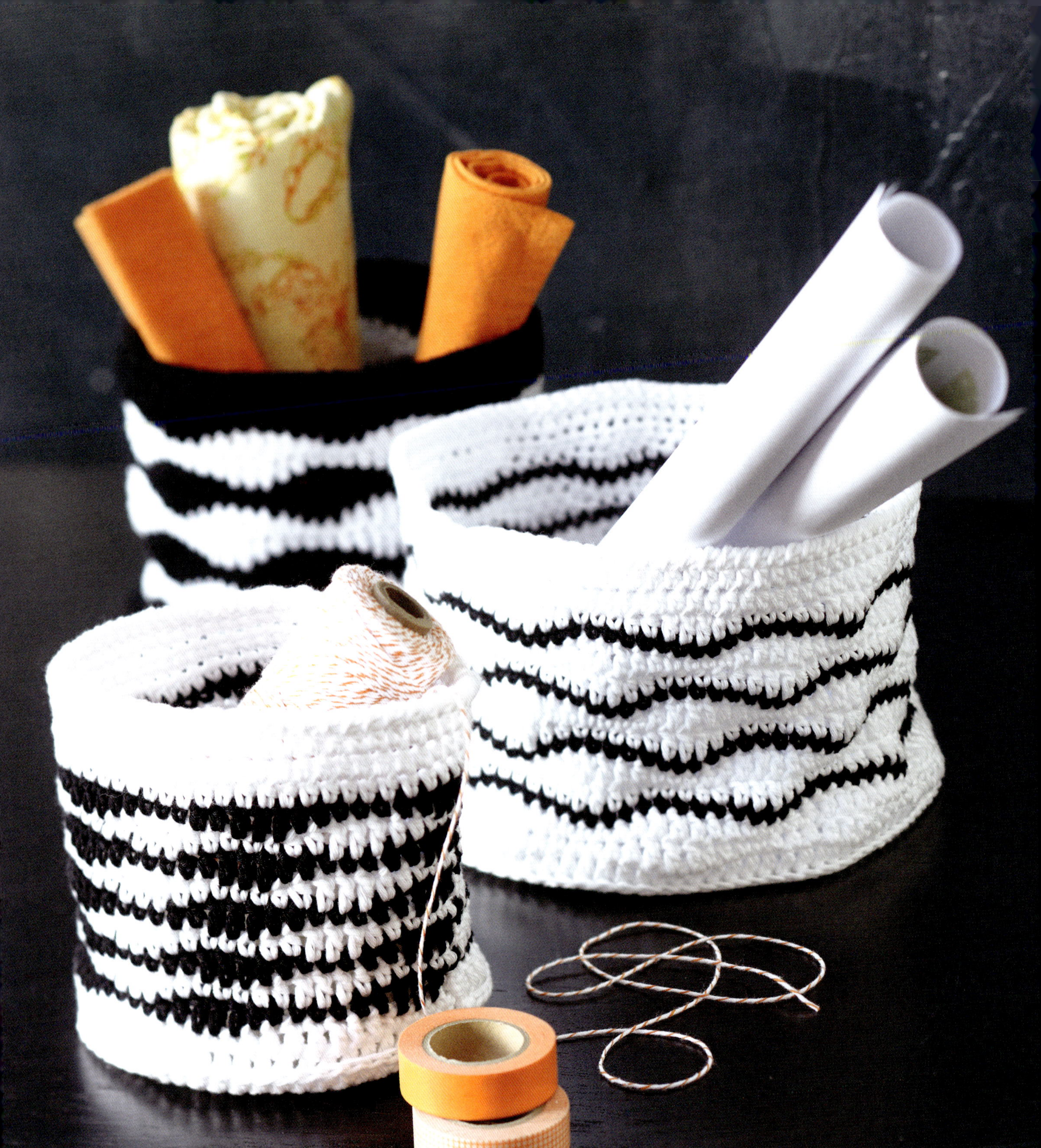

Rnd 9 (Black): (Hdc in next 7 sts, 2 hdc in next st) around (72 sts).

Rnd 10 (Black): (Hdc in next 8 sts, 2 hdc in next st) around (80 sts).

Rnds 11 and 12 (Black): Ch 1, hdc in each hdc around, join with sl st (80 sts).

Rnd 13 (Black): Ch 2, hdc in back loops around, join with sl st.

Rnd 14 (Black): Ch 1, hdc in each hdc around, join with sl st.

Rnds 15 and 16 (Black): Work as charted.

Rnds 17 and 18 (White): Work as charted.

Rnds 19–26: Rep Rnds 15–18.

Rnds 28 and 29 (Black): Ch 2, hdc in each st around, join with sl st.

LARGE BASKET

With White, make a magic ring.

Rnd 1 (White): Ch 2 and work 7 hdc in magic ring, join with sl st (8 sts).

Rnd 2 (White): 2 hdc in each st around (16 sts).

Rnd 3 (White): (Hdc in next st, 2 hdc in next st) around (24 sts).

Rnd 4 (White): (Hdc in next 2 sts, 2 hdc in next st) around (32 sts).

Rnd 5 (White): (Hdc in next 3 sts, 2 hdc in next st) around (40 sts).

Rnd 6 (White): (Hdc in next 4 sts, 2 hdc in next st) around (48 sts).

Rnd 7 (White): (Hdc in next 5 sts, 2 hdc in next st) around (56 sts).

Rnd 8 (White): (Hdc in next 6 sts, 2 hdc in next st) around (64 sts).

Rnd 9 (White): (Hdc in next 7 sts, 2 hdc in next st) around (72 sts).

Rnd 10 (White): (Hdc in next 8 sts, 2 hdc in next st) around (80 sts).

Rnd 11 (White): (Hdc in next 9 sts, 2 hdc in next st) around (80 sts).

Rnd 12 (White): (Hdc in next 10 sts, 2 hdc in next st) around (80 sts).

Rnd 13 (White): (Hdc in next 21 sts, 2 hdc in next st) 4 times, hdc to end (100 sts).

Rnd 14 (White): Ch 1, hdc in each hdc around, join with sl st (100 sts).

Rnd 15 (White): Ch 2, hdc in back loops around, join with sl st.

Rnds 16 and 17 (White): Work as charted.

Rnd 18 (Black): Work as charted.

Rnds 19 and 20 (White): Work as charted.

Rnd 21 (Black): Rep Rnd 18.

Rnds 22–27: Rep Rnds 16–21.

Rnd 28 (Black): Rep Rnd 16.

Rnds 29 and 30 (Black): Ch 2, hdc in each st around, join with sl st.

Rnds 28 and 29 (Black): Ch 2, hdc in each st around, join with sl st.

FINISHING (ALL BASKETS)

With color of last row, work 1 rnd in Crab Stitch. Weave in ends.

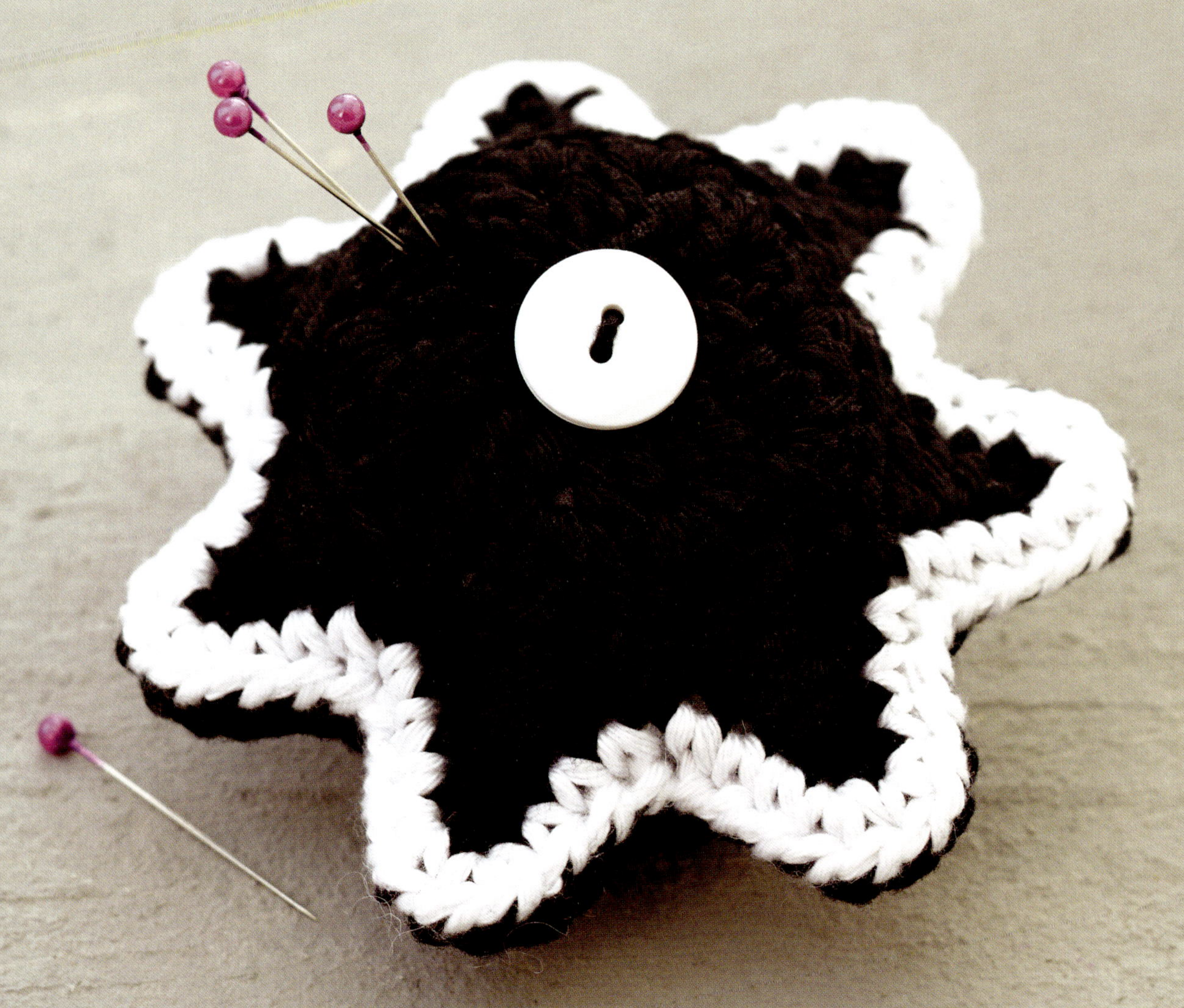

STARGAZER

A STAR-SHAPED PIN CUSHION

SKILL LEVEL

Intermediate

FINISHED MEASUREMENTS:

4¼ in / 11 cm across

MATERIALS

Yarn: CYCA #4 (worsted/afghan/aran), Schachenmayr Catania Grande or equivalent (100% cotton; 68 yd/62 m / 50 g)

Yarn Amounts:
White #3106, 50 g
Black #3110, 50 g

Hook: U.S. size G-6 / 4 mm

Notions: Tapestry needle, 1 black and 1 white button with ¼ in / 1 cm diameter, fiber fill stuffing, sewing needle and matching thread

Gauge: 18 sc and 18 rows = 4 x 4 in / 10 x 10 cm. Adjust needle size to obtain correct gauge if necessary.

INSTRUCTIONS

With White, make a magic loop.

Rnd 1: Ch 4, tr (1st Bobble), ch 1, *in the magic ring, tr2tog (2nd Bobble), ch 1; rep from * 8 more times (10 Bobbles). Join with sl st in first tr, work another sl st between 1st and 2nd Bobbles.

Rnd 2: Ch 2, 2 hdc in the first ch, sk the Bobble, 2 hdc in next ch, 3 hdc in each of the next 4 ch, 2 hdc in the next ch, 3 hdc in the next ch, join with sl st in the 2nd turning ch (28 sts).

Rnd 3: *Ch 5, sc in the 2nd ch from hk, hdc in next ch, dc in next ch, tr in last ch (1st point), skip the next 3 hdc of the prev rnd, sl st in the next st; rep from * 6 more times (7 points).

Rnd 4: Ch 1, sc in each st around, working 2 sc twice at each point, and join with sl st.

FINISHING

Make a second star with Black. Weave in ends. Sew contrasting button to center of each star. Place pieces together with RS facing out. Sew together around 5 points. Stuff, then sew together around remaining points. Bury last ends inside.

CLEVER SNAKE

STOP DRAFTS WITH FUN

SKILL LEVEL

Intermediate

FINISHED MEASUREMENTS:

41 in / 104 cm long

MATERIALS

Yarn: CYCA #6 (super bulky/roving) Schachenmayr Boston Sun or equivalent (50% acrylic, 50% cotton; 109 yd/100 m / 100 g), 200 g each of Black #99 and White #01
CYCA #3 (DK/light worsted), Schachenmayr Catania or equivalent (100% cotton; 137 yd/125 m / 50 g), small amount of Tomato #390

Hooks:
U.S. size H-8 / 5 mm
U.S. size B-1 / 2.5 mm

Notions: Tapestry needle, 2 safety eyes ½ in / 11 mm in diameter, fiber fill stuffing

Gauge: 13 sc and 16 rows = 4 x 4 in / 10 x 10 cm in Boston Sun with larger hook. Adjust needle size to obtain correct gauge if necessary.

INSTRUCTIONS

TONGUE

With Tomato and smaller hk, ch 4.

Row 1: Sc in 2nd ch from hk and each ch across (3 sts).

Rows 2–9: Ch 1 (turning ch), sc in each sc across.

Row 10: Ch 3, dc in first st, ch 2, sc in 2nd st, ch 3, dc in 3rd st, ch 2, sl st in 3rd st.

Fasten off.

HEAD

With White and larger hk, make a magic ring.

Rnd 1: Ch 1, 6 sc in magic ring, join with sl st (6 sts).

Rnd 2: 2 sc in each sc around (12 sts).

Rnd 3: (Sc in next sc, 2 sc in next sc) around (18 sts).

Rnd 4: (Sc in next 2 sc, 2 sc in next sc) around (24 sts).

Rnds 5 and 6: Ch 1, sc in each sc around, join with sl st.

Rnd 7: Ch 1, sc in next 4 sc, 2 sc in next sc, sc in next sc, 2 sc in next sc, sc in next 8 sc, 2 sc in next sc, sc in next sc, 2 sc in next sc, sc in next 5 sc, join with sl st (28 sts).

Rnd 8: Ch 1, sc in each sc around, join with sl st.

Rnd 9: Ch 1, sc in next 6 sc, 2 sc in next sc, sc in next sc, 2 sc in next sc, sc in each of next 10 sc, 2 sc in next sc, sc in next sc, 2 sc in next sc, sc in next 6 sc, join with sl st (32 sts).

Rnd 10: Ch 1, sc in each sc around, join with sl st.

Rnd 11: Ch 1, sc in next 7 sc, 2 sc in next sc, sc in next sc, 2 sc in next sc, sc in each of next 12

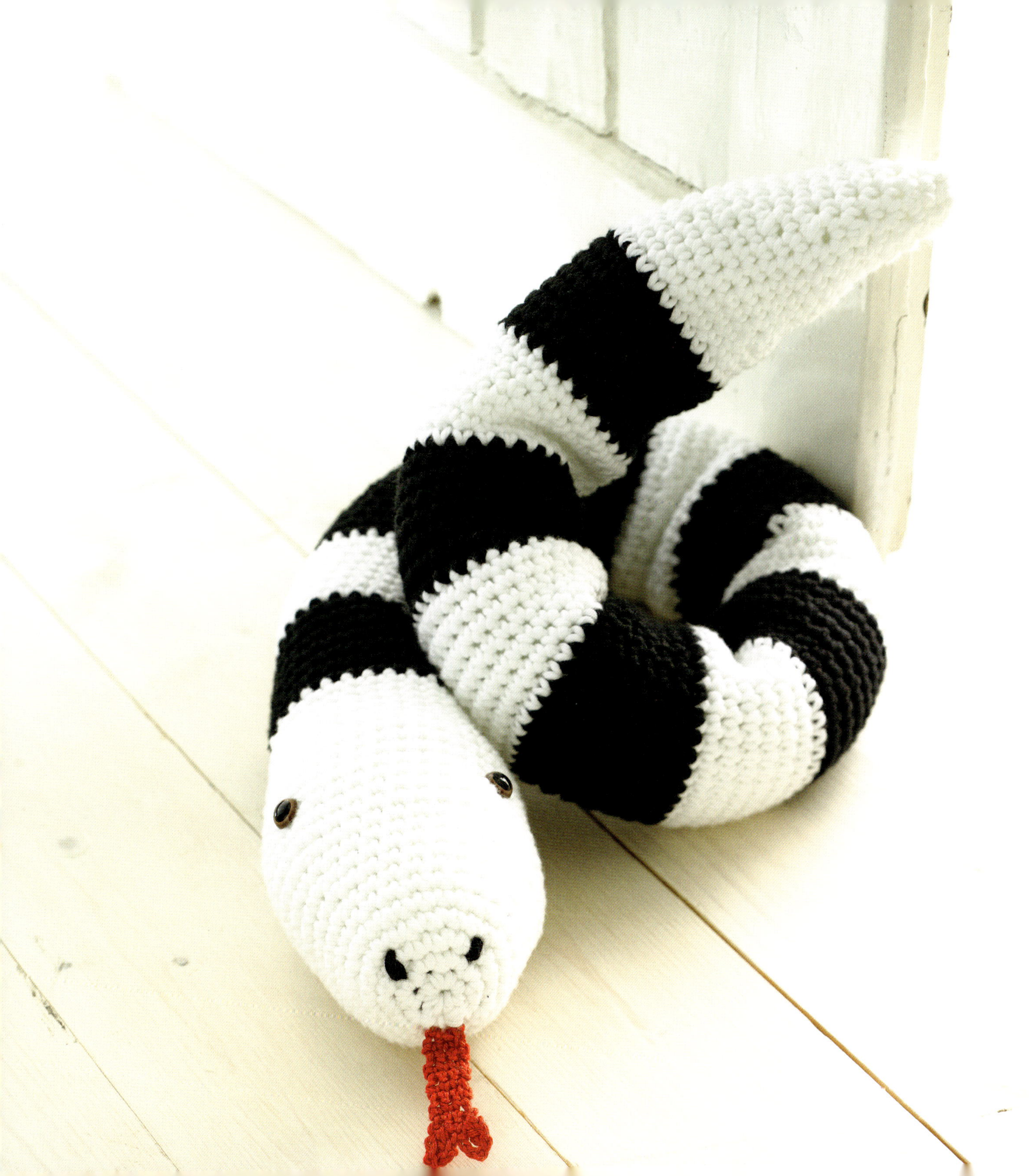

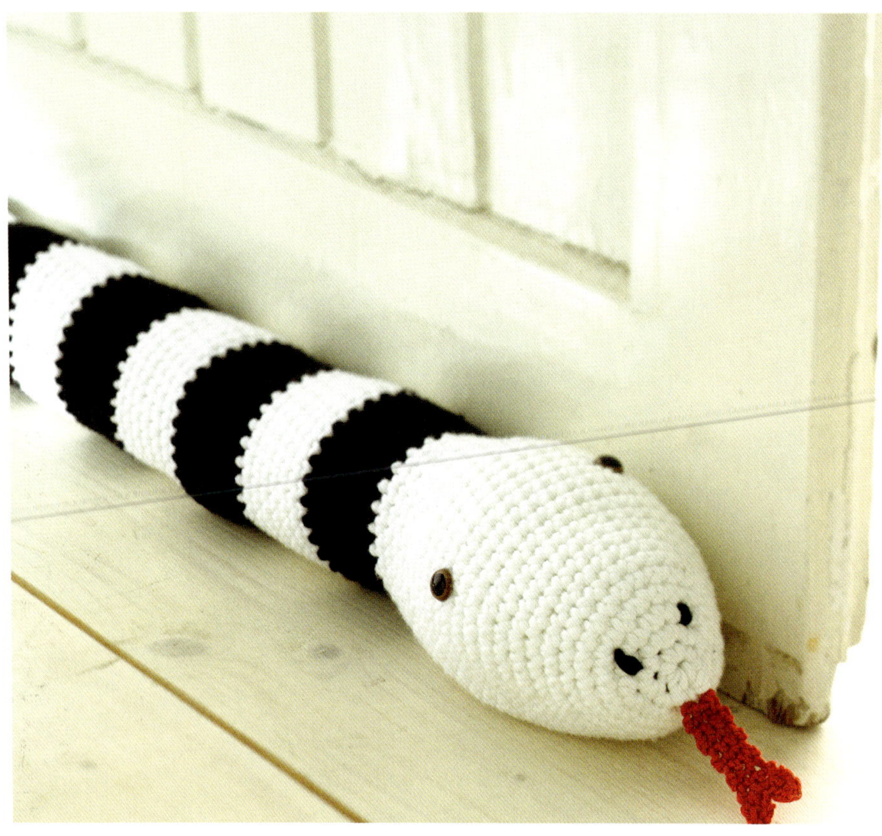

sc, 2 sc in next sc, sc in next sc, 2 sc in next sc, sc in next 7 sc, join with sl st (36 sts).

Rnds 12–18: Ch 1, sc in each sc around, join with sl st.

Rnd 19: (Sc in next 4 sc, sc2tog) around (30 sts).

Rnds 20 and 21: Ch 1, sc in each sc around, join with sl st.

Rnd 22: (Sc in next 8 sc, sc2tog) around (28 sts).

Rnds 23 and 24: Ch 1, sc in each sc around, join with sl st.

Using photo as a guide, attach the safety eyes and tongue, and embroider nose. Fill the head with fiber fill, and as you work the body, add stuffing every 8 to 10 rnds.

BODY

Every rnd begins with ch 1 and ends with a sl st to join.

Rnds 25–31 (Black): Sc in each sc around (27 sts).

Rnds 32–38 (White): Sc in each sc around.

Rnds 39–122: Rep Rnds 25–38 another 6 times.

TAIL

Work remainder of Snake in White.

Rnds 130–132: Sc in each sc around.

Rnd 133: (Sc in next 7 sc, sc2tog) around (24 sts).

Rnd 134: Sc in each sc around.

Rnd 135: (Sc in next 6 sc, sc2tog) around (21 sts).

Rnd 136: Sc in each sc around.

Rnd 137: (Sc in next 5 sc, sc2tog) around (18 sts)

Rnd 138: Sc in each sc around.

Rnd 139: (Sc in next 4 sc, sc2tog) around (15 sts).

Rnd 140: Sc in each sc around.

Rnd 141: (Sc in next 3 sc, sc2tog) around (12 sts).

Rnd 142: Sc in each sc around.

Rnd 143: (Sc in next 2 sc, sc2tog) around (9 sts).

Rnds 144 and 145: Sc in each sc around.

Cut yarn, leaving a tail 6 in / 15 cm long.

FINISHING

Use the tail to gather in the last 9 sts and fasten off. Weave in ends.

WASHROOM FUN

CUTE ACCESSORIES FOR THE BATH

SKILL LEVEL

Intermediate

TOILET PAPER COVER

FINISHED MEASUREMENTS:

4 in / 10.5 cm tall, 5½ in / 14 cm diameter

MATERIALS

Yarn: CYCA #6 (super bulky/roving) Schachenmayr Boston or equivalent (70% acrylic, 30% wool; 131 yd/120 m / 200 g)

Yarn Amounts:
Black #99, 50 g
White #101, 50 g

Hook: U.S. size J-10 / 6 mm

Notions: Tapestry needle

TOILET SEAT COVER

FINISHED MEASUREMENTS:

20½ in / 52 cm in diameter

MATERIALS

Yarn: CYCA #6 (super bulky/roving) Schachenmayr Boston or equivalent (70% acrylic, 30% wool; 131 yd/120 m / 200 g)

Yarn Amounts:
Black #99, 50 g
White #101, 50 g

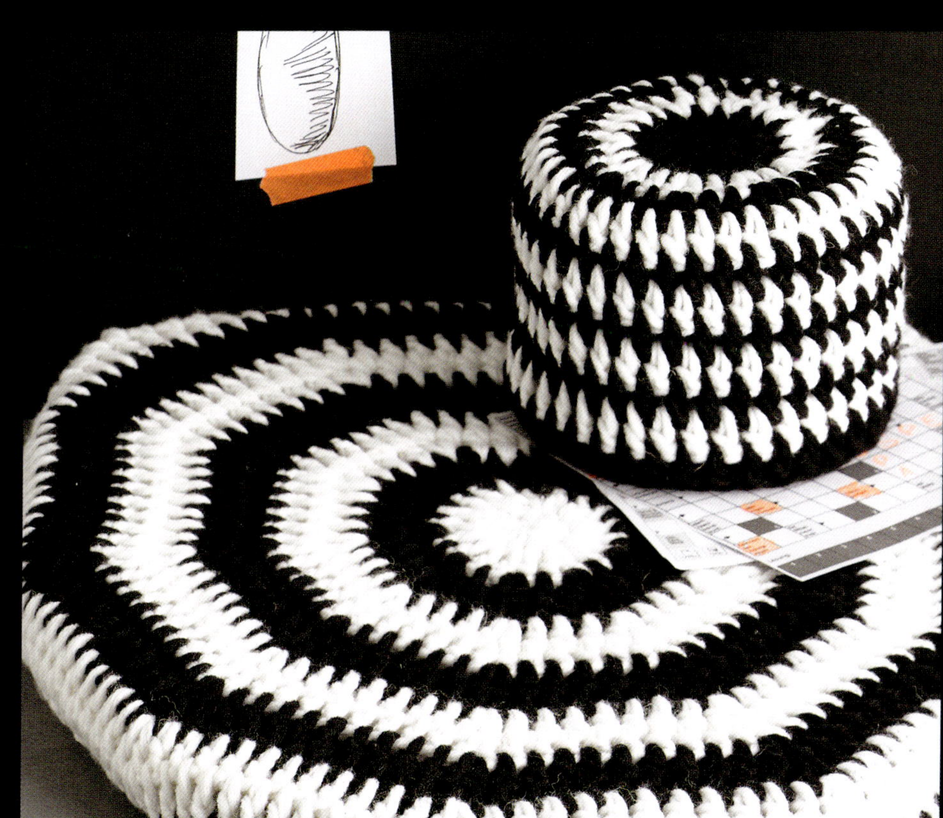

Hook: U.S. size J-10 / 6 mm

Notions: Tapestry needle

Gauge: 16 sc and 17 rows = 4 x 4 in / 10 x 10 cm. Adjust needle size to obtain correct gauge if necessary.

TOILET PAPER COVER

Worked in the round with elongated dc. Each rnd begins with ch 3 (counts as 1 dc) and ends with a slip st in the 3rd ch.

With Black, make a magic ring.

Rnd 1 (Black): Ch 3 (counts as dc), 9 dc in magic ring, join with sl st (10 sts). Begin and end each following rnd the same way, unless otherwise indicated.

Rnd 2 (Black): Work elongated dc in first dc, work 2 elongated dc in each dc around (20 sts).

Rnd 3 (White): (Elongated dc in next st, 2 elongated dc in next st) around (30 sts).

Rnd 4 (Black): (Elongated dc in next 2 sts, 2 elongated dc in next st) around (40 sts).

Rnd 5 (White): Elongated dc in each st around (40 sts).

Rnd 6 (Black): Elongated dc in each st around (40 sts).

Rnds 7–12: Change colors and rep Rnds 5 and 6.

Rnd 13 (Black): Ch 1, sc in each st around, join with sl st (40 sts).

FINISHING

Weave in ends.

TOILET SEAT COVER

STRIPE PATTERN

*Work 2 rnds in White, work 2 rnds in Black; rep from * for stripe pattern.

INSTRUCTIONS

Worked in the round with elongated dc. Each rnd begins with ch 3 (counts as 1 dc) and ends with a slip st in the 3rd ch.

With White, make a magic ring.

Rnd 1: Ch 3 (counts as dc), 9 dc in magic ring, join with sl st (10 sts). Begin and end each following rnd the same way.

Rnd 2: Work elongated dc in first dc, work 2 elongated dc in each dc around (20 sts).

Rnd 3: (Elongated dc in next st, 2 elongated dc in next st) around (30 sts).

Rnd 4: (Elongated dc in next 2 sts, 2 elongated dc in next st) around (40 sts).

Rnd 5: (Elongated dc in next 3 sts, 2 elongated dc in next st) around (50 sts).

Rnds 6–15: Continue increasing 10 sts per round in the same fashion.

Rnd 16: Elongated dc in each st around (150 sts).

CORD

With Black, make a chain 65 in / 165 cm long.

FINISHING

Weave in ends. Weave the cord through the top edge, going in and out of the crochet 3 stitches apart, starting and ending on the outside of the seat cover, leaving 8 in / 20 cm free at the end. Gather the seat cover around the seat, tie the cords, and adjust the length if necessary.

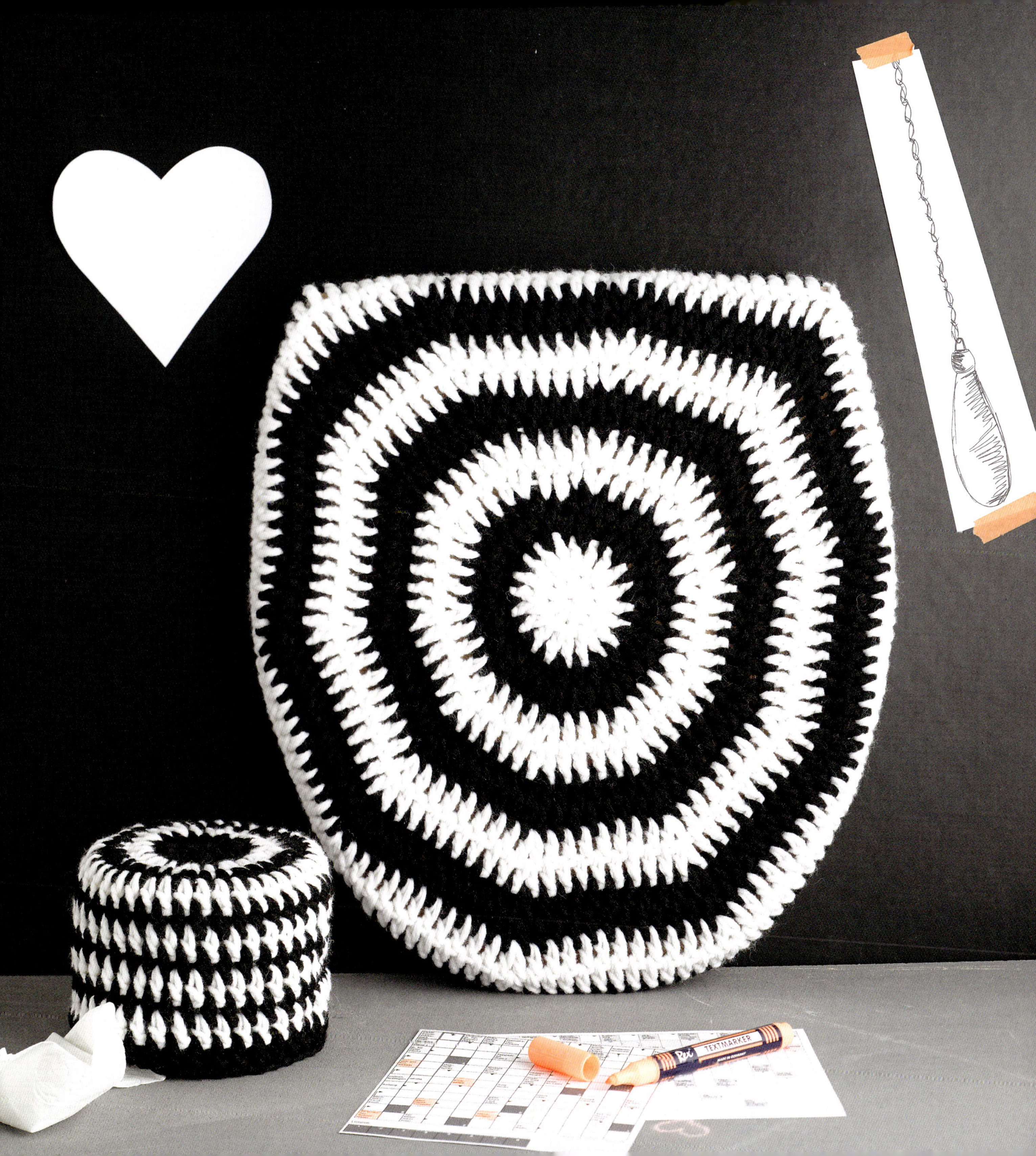
Rei
TEXTMARKER
MADE IN GERMANY

WASHNG DAY

HANGING LAUNDRY BASKET

SKILL LEVEL

Easy

FINISHED MEASUREMENTS:

12 in / 31 cm diameter, 14 in / 36 cm tall

MATERIALS

Yarn: Woll Butt Textilgarn or equivalent (95% cotton, 5% other; 76 yd/69 m / 450 g) in Black & White Combo, 2 cones.

Hook: U.S. size L-11 / 8 mm

Notions: Tapestry needle

Gauge: 8 sc and 10 rnds = 4 x 4 in / 10 x 10 cm. Adjust needle size to obtain correct gauge if necessary.

INSTRUCTIONS

Worked in the round in sc. Each rnd begins with ch 1 and ends with a sl st to join to the 1st sc.

Make a magic ring.

Rnd 1: Ch 1, 8 sc in magic ring, join with sl st (8 sts). Begin and end each following Rnd the same way.

Rnd 2: 2 sc in each sc around (16 sts).

Rnd 3: (Sc in next sc, 2 sc in next sc) around (24 sts).

Rnd 4: (Sc in next 2 sc, 2 sc in next sc) around (32 sts).

Rnd 5: (Sc in next 3 sc, 2 sc in next sc) around (40 sts).

Rnd 6: (Sc in next 4 sc, 2 sc in next sc) around (48 sts).

Rnd 7: (Sc in next 5 sc, 2 sc in next sc) around (56 sts).

Rnd 8: (Sc in next 6 sc, 2 sc in next sc) around (64 sts).

Rnd 9: (Sc in next 7 sc, 2 sc in next sc) around (72 sts).

Rnd 10: (Sc in next 8 sc, 2 sc in next sc) around (80 sts).

Rnds 11–36: 2 sc in next st, *sk next st, 2 sc in next st; rep from * around (80 sts).

Rnd 37: 2 sc in next st, (sk next st, 2 sc in next st) twice, sk next st, insert into next st and draw up a lp, sk next st, insert hook into next st and draw up a lp, sk next st, yo hk and draw through all 3 lps together, sc in same st, * (sk the next st, 2 sc in next st) 3 times, sk next st, insert into next st and draw up a lp, sk next st, insert hook into next st and draw up a lp, sk next st, yo hk and draw through all 3 lps together, sc in same st; rep from * around (64 sts).

Rnd 38: Work as for Rnd 37, decreasing in the same fashion (48 sts).

Rnds 39 and 40: Rep Rnd 11.

FINISHING

Work 1 rnd of crab stitch.

For the handle, ch 30, join with sl st to 1st ch. Turn. Sc in each ch across. Turn. Sc in each sc across. Sc to attach handle to bag. Cut yarn. Use the tail to secure the spot where the handle attaches to the bag with several sewn reinforcement stitches.

Weave in ends.

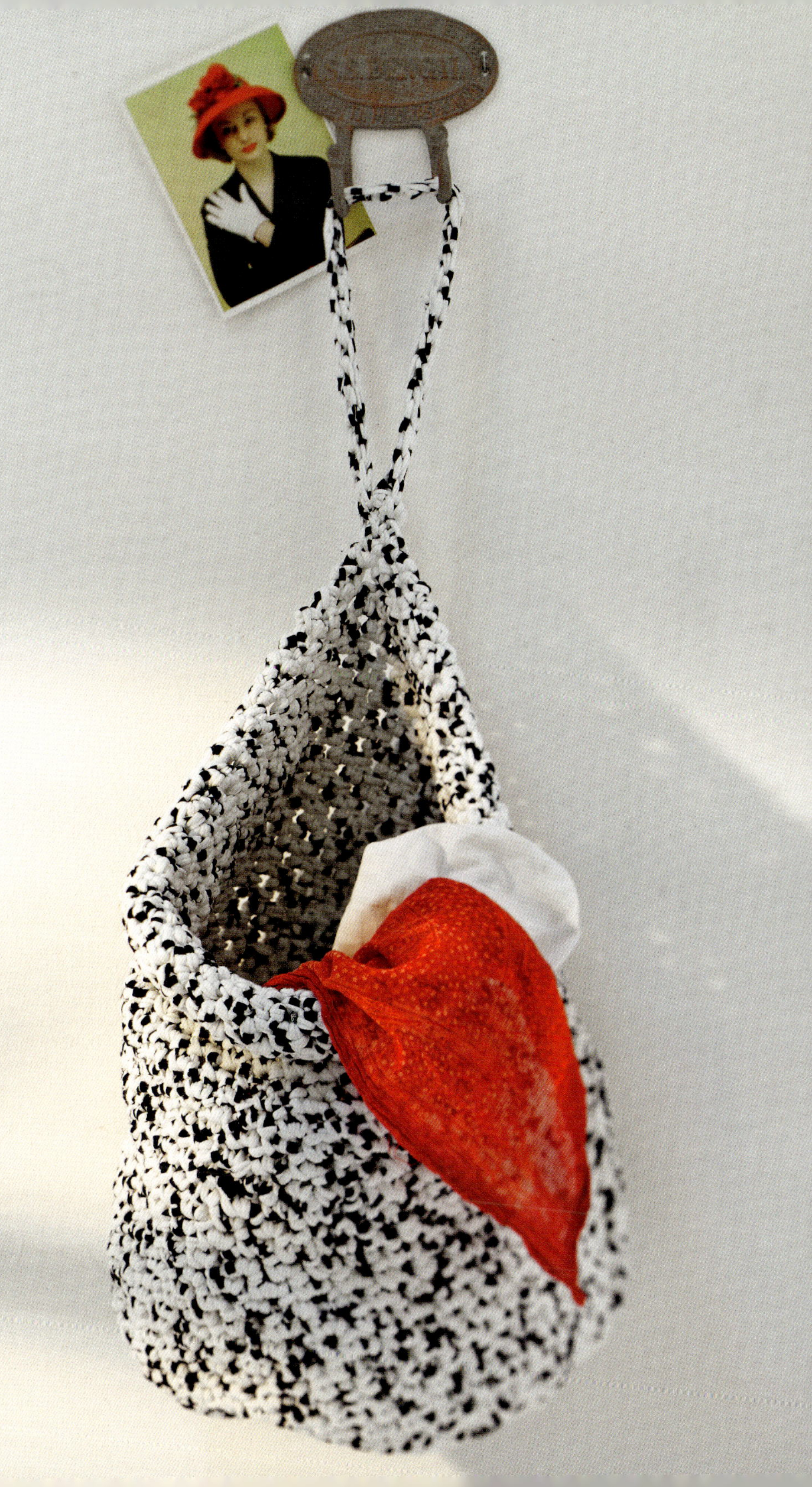

KITCHEN PIRATES

POTHOLDERS WITH SKULLS

SKILL LEVEL

Easy

FINISHED MEASUREMENTS:

8¼ x 8¼ in / 21 x 21 cm

MATERIALS

Yarn: CYCA #4 (worsted/afghan/aran), Schachenmayr Catania Grande or equivalent (100% cotton; 68 yd/62 m / 50 g)

Yarn Amounts:
Black #3110, 100 g
White #3106, 50 g

Hook: U.S. size G-6 / 4 mm

Notions: Tapestry needle

Gauge: 18 sc and 16 rows = 4 x 4 in / 10 x 10 cm. Adjust needle size to obtain correct gauge if necessary.

Chart: Page 95

INSTRUCTIONS

With Black, ch 33.

Row 1: Sc in 2nd ch from hk and in each ch across (32 sc).

Rows 2–33: Ch 1 (turning ch), follow chart across next 32 sts.

Do not cut yarn.

LOOP AND BORDER

Work in rnds for the loop and border.

Rnd 1: Ch 1, 2 sc in corner st, sc in each st along side of potholder, 3 sc in next corner, sc in each sc along edge, 3 sc in next corner, sc in each st along other side of potholder, 3 sc in next corner, sc in each sc along edge, sc in first st (last st of first corner), join with sl st in the first loop (134 sts).

Rnd 2: Ch 1, sc in the first corner st, * sc in each sc across the side, 3 sc in corner st; rep from * 2 more times, ch 15 for loop, sc in the same sc worked before the loop chain, sc in each sc across final side, sc in the last sc (last st of first corner), join with sl st in first lp (142 sts).

FINISHING

Weave in ends.

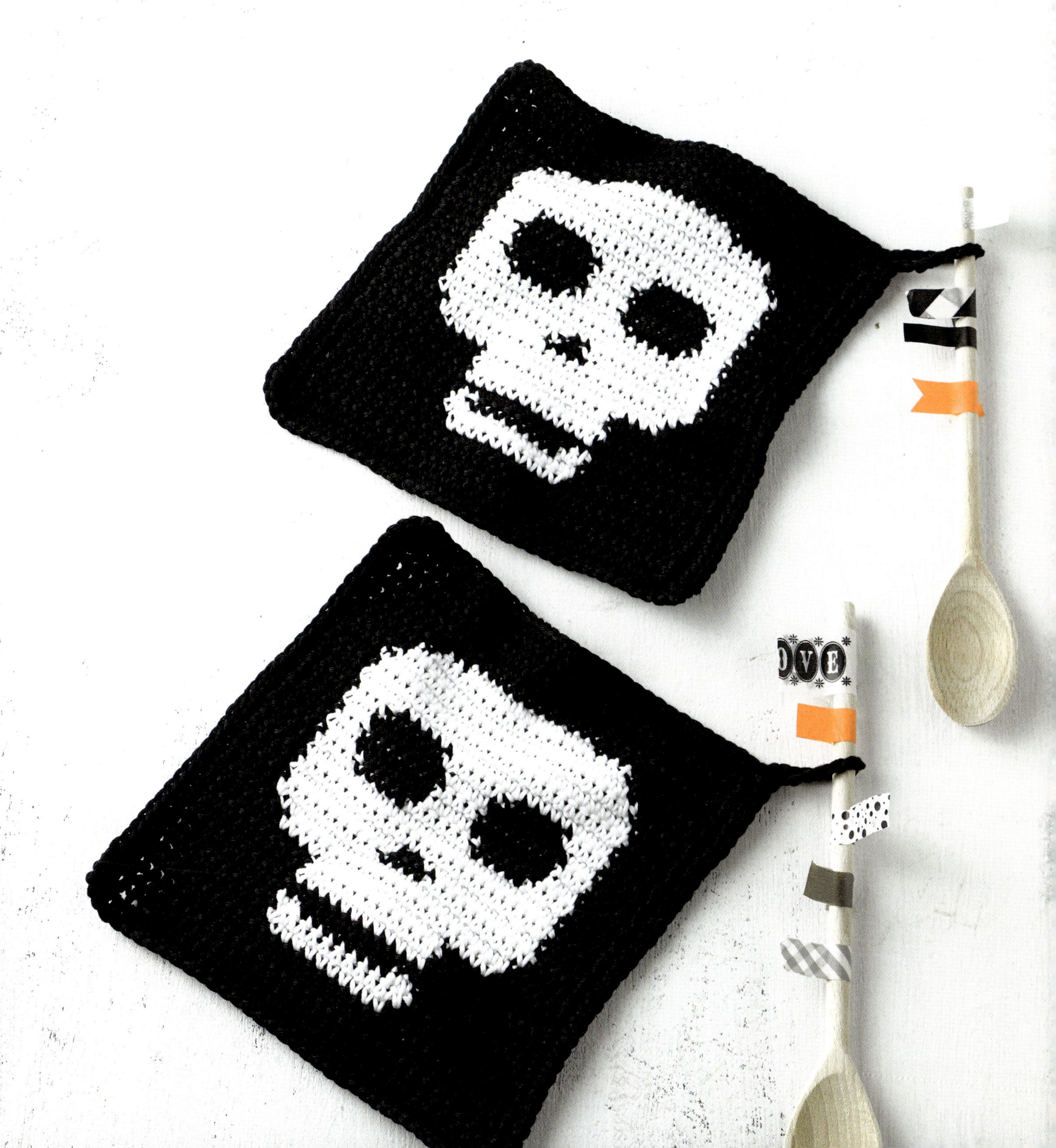

TABLE LINENS JUST FOR YOU

PRACTICAL TABLE SETTING

SKILL LEVEL

Easy

PLACEMATS

FINISHED MEASUREMENTS:

16½ x 12 in / 42 x 31 cm

MATERIALS

Yarn: CYCA #4 (worsted/afghan/aran), Schachenmayr Catania Grande or equivalent (100% cotton; 68 yd/62 m / 50 g)

Yarn Amounts: Black #3110, 250 g

Hooks:
U.S. size 7 / 4.5 mm
U.S. size E-4 / 3.5 mm

Notions: Tapestry needle, 2 white buttons ½ in / 15 mm in diameter, sewing needle and matching thread

Gauge: 18 sts (6 repeats) and 18 rows = 4 x 4 in / 10 x 10 cm in Pattern Stitch with larger hook. Adjust needle size to obtain correct gauge if necessary.

COASTER

FINISHED MEASUREMENTS:

4½ x 4½ in / 11.5 x 11.5 cm

MATERIALS

Yarn: CYCA #4 (worsted/afghan/aran), Schachenmayr Catania Grande or equivalent (100% cotton; 68 yd/62 m / 50 g)

Yarn Amounts: Black #3110, 25 g

Hook: U.S. size G-6 / 4 mm

Notions: Tapestry needle, 4 white buttons ½ in (15 mm) in diameter, sewing needle and matching thread

Gauge: 15 dc and 7 rows = 4 x 4 in / 10 x 10 cm. Adjust needle size to obtain correct gauge if necessary.

Chart: Page 100

PLACEMATS

PATTERN STITCH

Row 1: Ch 1 (turning ch), ch 1, sk 1 st, * 2 sc in next st, ch 1, sk 2 sts; rep from * across, sc in last st.

Row 2: Ch 1 (turning ch), ch 1, sk first st, * 2 sc in next ch sp, ch 1; rep from * across, sc in last st.

Rep Row 2 for pattern.

INSTRUCTIONS

With larger hk, ch 48.

Row 1: Sc in 2nd ch from hk and each ch across (47 sts).

Rows 2–60: Work in Pattern Stitch.

Row 61: Ch 1 (turning ch), sc in each sc and ch sp across, 2 sc in last ch sp (47 sts).

Do not cut yarn.

BORDER

Change to smaller hk and work in rnds.

Rnd 1: Ch 1, 2 sc in first corner st, sc in each st along side edge of mat, 3 sc in next corner st,

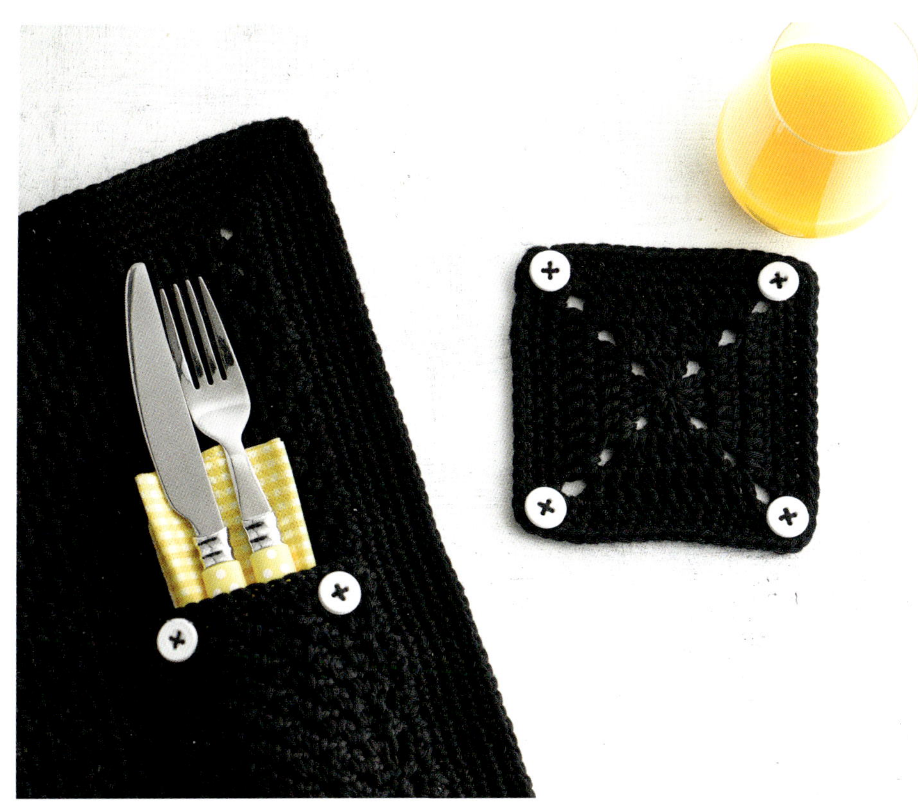

sc in each sc along bottom of mat, 3 sc in next corner st, sc in each st along second side of mat, 3 sc in next corner st, sc across top of mat, sc in last corner (this is the last st of first corner), join wth sl st (220 sts).

Rnd 2: Do not work a turning ch, begin with 2 sc in first st so all corners match, place marker for beg of rnd, * sc in each sc along edge of mat, 3 sc in corner; rep from * 2 more times, sc in each sc across last side of mat, sc in last corner (there are now 3 sc in this corner), join with sl st (228 sts).

Rnds 3 and 4: Rep Rnd 2.

Cut yarn.

POCKET

The long sides of the mat are the top and bottom. At the bottom of the mat, count six stitches in from the right edge. Join yarn here and work in rows.

Row 1: Ch 1 (turning ch), sc in next 17 sts of the bottom edge of the mat (17 sts).

Rows 2–20: Work in Pattern Stitch.

Row 21: Ch 1 (turning ch), sc in each st across.

FINISHING

Sew the sides of the pocket to the placemat. Sew on buttons as shown in photo. Weave in ends.

COASTERS

Make a magic ring.

Rnds 1–3: Work as charted.

BORDER

Join yarn in a corner.

Rnd 1: Ch 1, 2 sc in corner st, * sc in each sc across side, 3 sc in corner st; rep from * 2 more times, sc in each sc across last side, sc in last corner (corner now has 3 sts), join with sl st (56 sts).

Rnd 2: Ch 1, 2 sc in first corner, * sc in each sc across side, 3 sc in corner st; rep from * 2 more times, sc in each sc across last side, sc in last corner (corner now has 3 sts), join with sl st (64 sts).

Rnds 3 and 4: Rep Rnd 2.

FINISHING

Weave in ends. Sew on buttons.

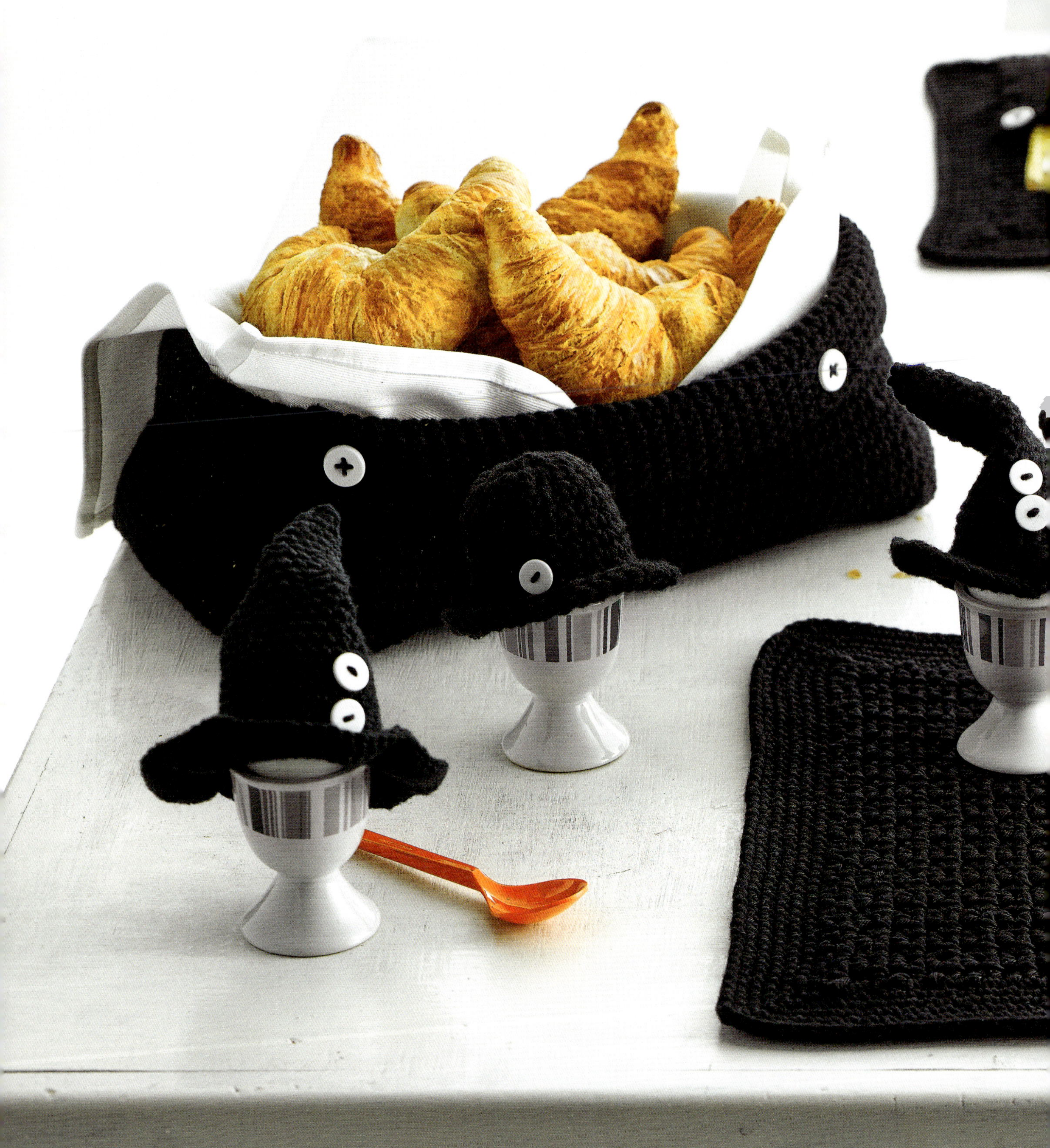

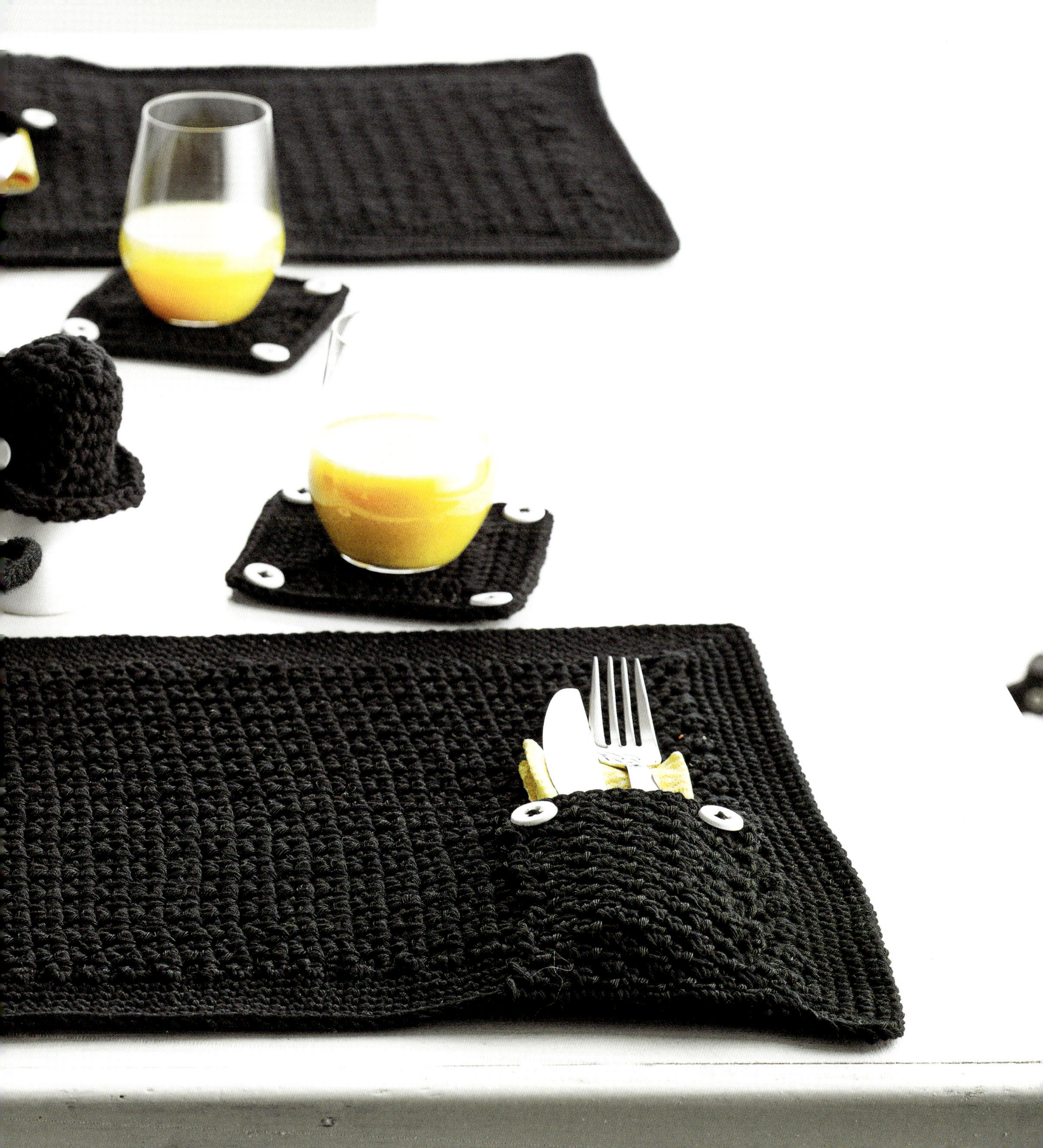

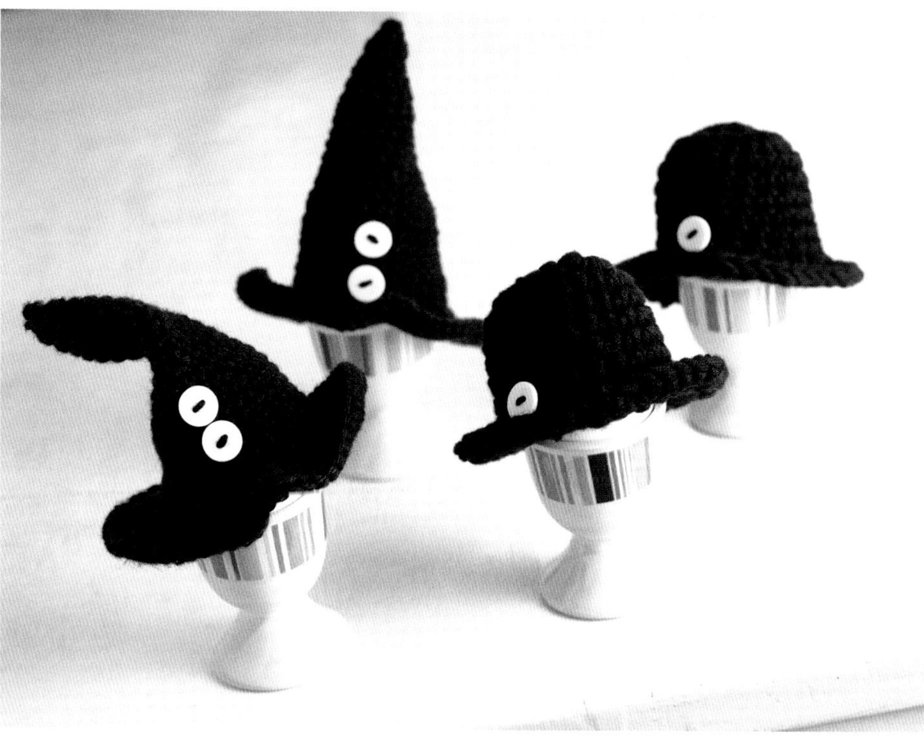

EGG WARMER HAT

FINISHED MEASUREMENTS:

2¼ in / 6 cm tall, 4 in / 10 cm diameter at widest point

MATERIALS

Yarn: CYCA #6 (super bulky/roving) Schachenmayr Boston Sun or equivalent (50% acrylic, 50% cotton; 109 yd/100 m / 100 g)

Yarn Amounts:
Black #99, 50 g

Hook: U.S. size H-8 / 5 mm

Notions: Tapestry needle, white button ½ in / 12 mm in diameter, sewing needle and matching thread

Gauge: 13 sc and 16 rows = 4 x 4 in / 10 x 10 cm. Adjust needle size to obtain correct gauge if necessary.

EGG WARMER WITCH'S HAT

FINISHED MEASUREMENTS:

4 in / 10 cm tall, 4 in / 10 cm diameter at widest point

MATERIALS

Yarn: CYCA #4 (worsted/afghan/aran), Schachenmayr Cotton Time or equivalent (100% cotton; 96 yd/88 m / 50 g)

Yarn Amounts: Black #99, 50 g

Hook: U.S. size E-4 / 3.5 mm

Notions: Tapestry needle, 2 white buttons ½ in / 12 mm in diameter, stitch marker, sewing needle and matching thread

Gauge: 16 sc and 17 rows = 4 x 4 in / 10 x 10 cm. Adjust needle size to obtain correct gauge if necessary.

BREAD BASKET

FINISHED MEASUREMENTS:

Bottom 12 x 5½ in / 30 x 14 cm, 3¾ in / 9 cm tall

MATERIALS

Yarn: CYCA #6 (super bulky/roving) Schachenmayr Boston Sun or equivalent (50% acrylic, 50% cotton; 109 yd/100 m / 100 g)

Yarn Amounts: Black #99, 300 g

Hook: U.S. size H-8 / 5 mm

Notions: Tapestry needle, 4 white buttons ½ in / 15 mm in diameter, sewing needle and matching thread

Gauge: 13 sc and 16 rows = 4 x 4 in / 10 x 10 cm. Adjust needle size to obtain correct gauge if necessary.

EGG WARMER HAT

Hat is worked in rounds. Each round begins with a turning chain and ends with a slip stitch to join.

Make a magic ring.

Rnd 1: Ch 2, 9 hdc in magic ring, join with sl st (10 sts).

Rnd 2: Ch 1, 2 sc in each st around, join with sl st (20 sts).

Rnds 3-6: Ch 1, sc in each sc around, join with sl st (20 sts).

Rnd 7: (Sc in next st, 2 sc in next st) around (30 sts).

Rnd 8: (Sc in next 2 st, 2 sc in next st) around (40 sts).

FINISHING

Weave in ends and sew on button.

EGG WARMER WITCH'S HAT

Hat is worked in spiral rounds. Use a marker to keep track of ends of rounds.

Ch 28 and join with sl st to form a ring.

Rnds 1-6: Sc in each st around (28 sts).

Rnd 7: (5 sc, sc2tog) around (24 sts).

Rnd 8: Sc in each st around.

Rnd 9: (4 sc, sc2tog) around (20 sts).

Rnds 10 and 11: Sc in each st around.

Rnd 12: (3 sc, sc2tog) around (16 sts).

Rnds 13 and 14: Sc in each st around.

Rnd 15: (2 sc, sc2tog) around (12 sts).

Rnds 16 and 17: Sc in each st around.

Rnd 18: (1 sc, sc2tog) around (8 sts).

Rnds 19 and 20: Sc in each st around.

Rnds 21-23: (sc2tog) around (1 sts).

At the top make 1 dc through both layers to close the top.

BRIM

Work into bottom of foundation chain. Each rnd begins with a turning ch and ends with a sl st to join.

Rnd 1: Ch 1, sc in each st around, join with sl st (28 sts).

Rnd 2: (Sc in next sc, 2 sc in next st) around (42 sts).

Rnd 3: (Sc in next 2 sc, 2 sc in next st) around (56 sts).

Rnd 4: (Sc in next 3 sc, 2 sc in next st) around (70 sts).

Rnds 5 and 6: Ch 1, sc in each sc around, join with sl st.

FINISHING

Weave in ends and sew on buttons.

BREAD BASKET

BOTTOM

Ch 40.

Row 1: Sc in 2nd ch from hk and in each ch across (39 sts).

Rows 2–22: Ch 1 (turning ch), sc in each sc across.

Do not cut yarn.

SIDES

Work in rnds, crocheting around all 4 sides of bottom to complete 1 rnd. The last stitch of one side is also the first stitch of the next side, as well as being counted as the corner stitch.

Rnd 1: Ch 1, sc in the first corner-st, 20 sc, 1 sc in the 2nd corner st, 37 sc, 1 sc in the 3rd corner st, 20 sc, 1 sc in the 4th corner st, 38 sc, join with sl st (118 sts).

Rnd 2: Ch 1, sc2tog, * sc across to next corner, after the corner st, sc2tog; rep from * 2 more times, sc in each sc to end of rnd, join with sl st (114 sts).

Rnd 3: Rep Rnd 2 (110 sts).

Rnds 4 and 5: Ch 1, sc in each sc around, join with sl st.

Rnd 6: Rep Rnd 2 (106 sts).

Rnds 7 and 8: Ch 1, sc in each sc around, join with sl st.

Rnd 9: Rep Rnd 2 (102 sts).

Rnds 10-22: Ch 1, sc in each sc around, join with sl st.

FINISHING

Weave in ends. Fold the top edge down and sew on the buttons.

JOURNEY

A BASKET FOR TOYS OR PETS

SKILL LEVEL

Easy

FINISHED MEASUREMENTS:

17 in / 43 cm diameter, 4¼ in / 10.5 cm tall

MATERIALS

Yarn: Woll Butt Textilgarn 1 in / 3 cm or equivalent (95% cotton, 5% other; 76 yd/69 m / 450 g)

Yarn Amounts:
Black, 1 cone
White, 1 cone

Hook: U.S. size N/P-15 / 10 mm

Notions: Tapestry needle

Gauge: 6 sc and 8 rows = 4 x 4 in / 10 x 10 cm. Adjust needle size to obtain correct gauge if necessary.

STRIPE PATTERN

*Work 3 rnds in White then 2 rnds in Black; rep from * for stripe patt.

INSTRUCTIONS

Worked in the rnd in stripe pattern. Each rnd begins with 1 turning ch and ends with a sl st to join.

With White, make a magic ring.

Rnd 1: Ch 1, 9 sc in magic ring, join with sl st (9 sts).

Rnd 2: 2 sc in each sc around (18 sts).

Rnd 3: (Sc in next 2 sc, 2 sc in next sc) around (24 sts).

Rnd 4: (Sc in next 3 sc, 2 sc in next sc) around (30 sts).

Rnd 5: (Sc in next 4 sc, 2 sc in next sc) around (36 sts).

Rnd 6: (Sc in next 5 sc, 2 sc in next sc) around (42 sts).

Rnd 7: (Sc in next 6 sc, 2 sc in next sc) around (48 sts).

Rnd 8: (Sc in next 7 sc, 2 sc in next sc) around (54 sts).

Beginning with Rnd 9, continue to work in stripe pattern and increase 6 sts in each rnd as above until work measures 15¾ in / 40 cm. If the bottom of the basket starts to ruffle up, work 1 rnd with no increasing.

SIDES

Work 7 rnds without increasing, continuing stripe pattern. Change to White and continue to work with no increases until basket is 4 in / 10 cm tall.

FINISHING

Cut a piece of Black 63 in / 160 cm long and thread it onto a tapestry needle. Work overhand stitch around the edge of the basket, going into every 4th sc. When you reach the beginning, bury the yarn ends. Weave in all other ends.

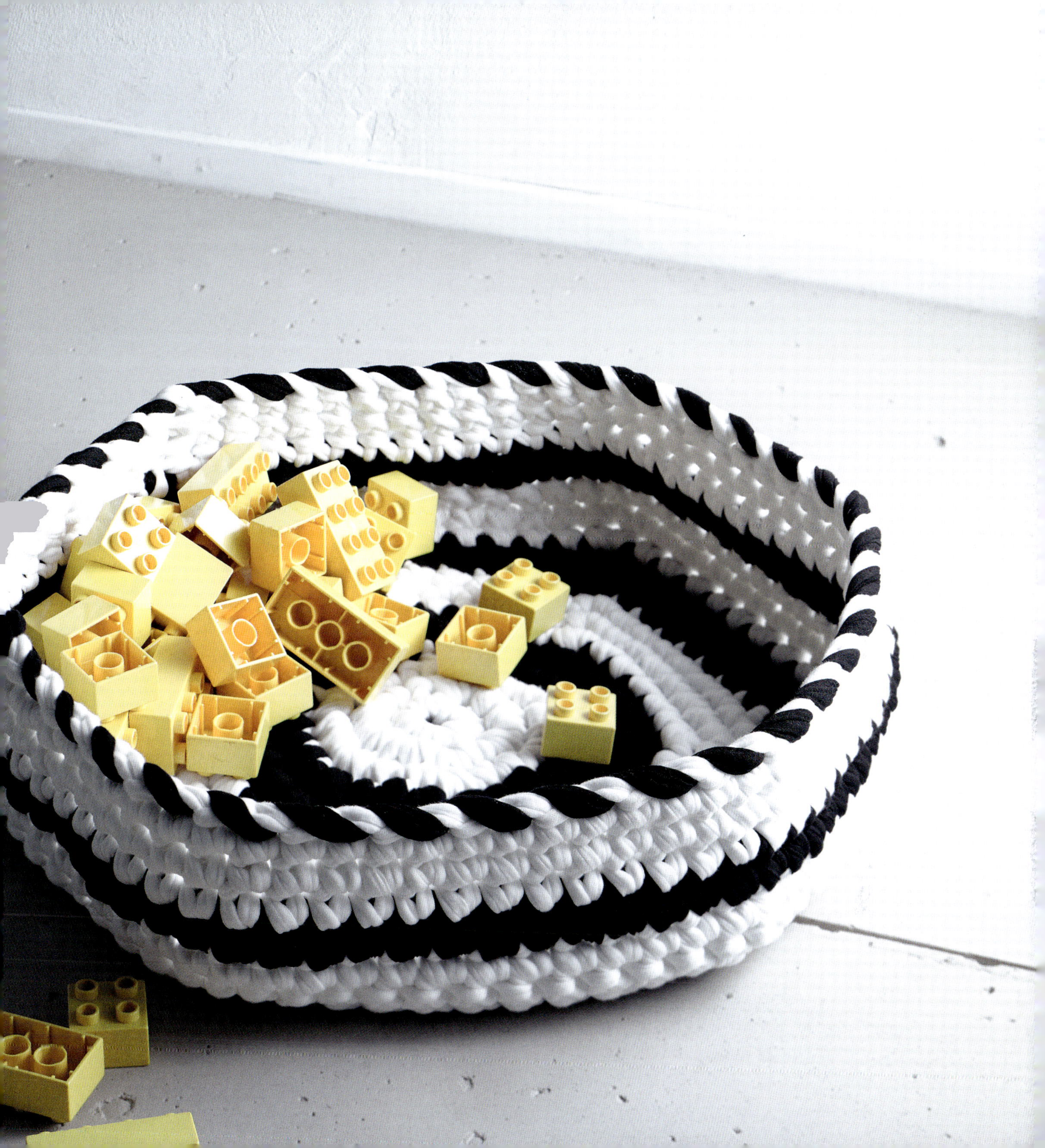

SKYLINE

Page 18

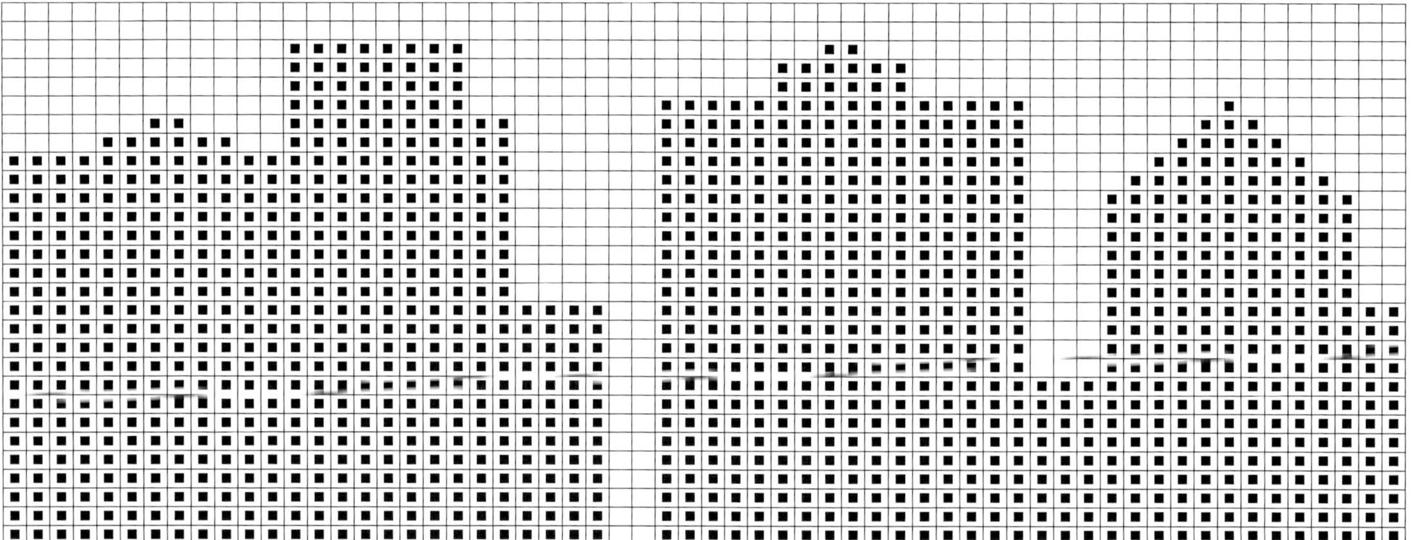

Pattern = 108 sts

MUSIC IS MY FIRST LOVE

Page 6

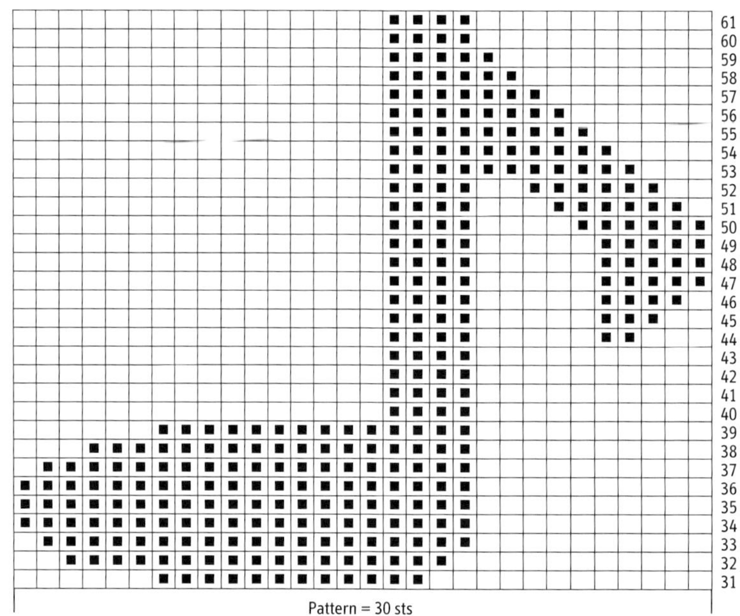

Pattern = 30 sts

☐ = White
■ = Black

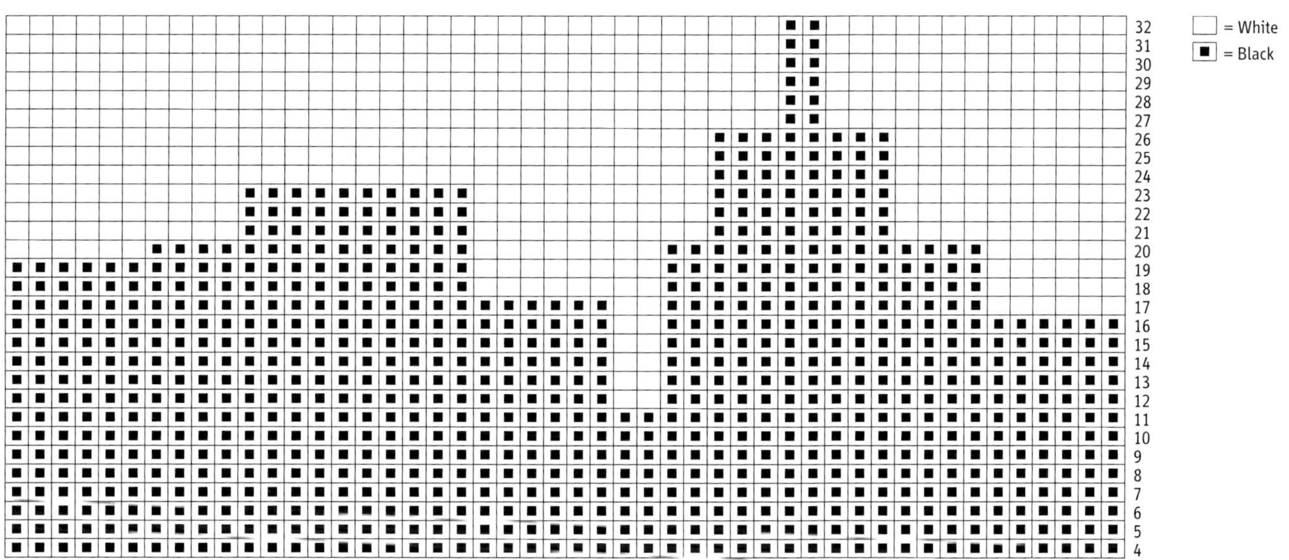

KITCHEN PIRATES

Page 84

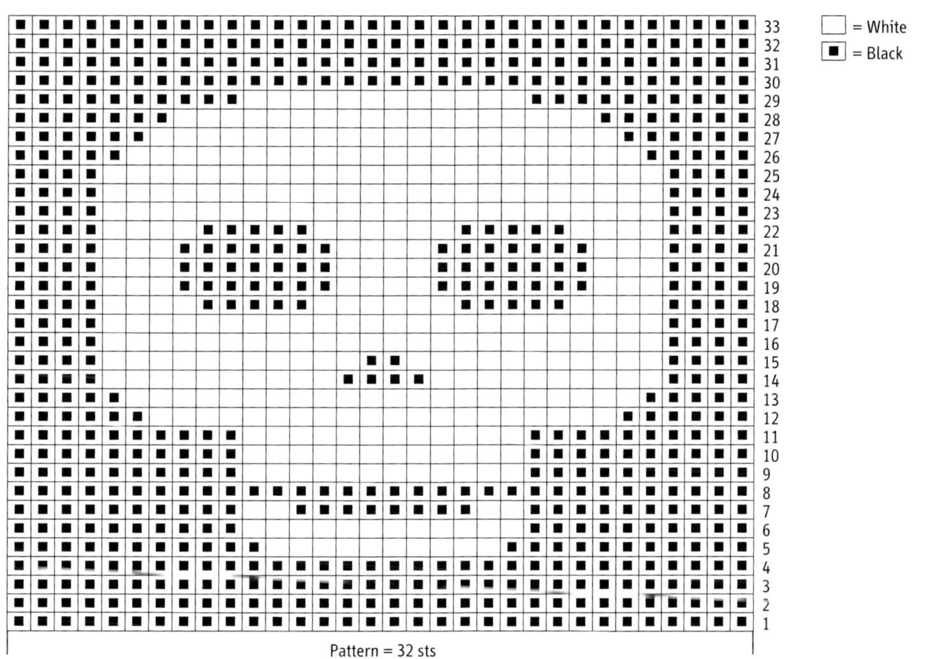

STYLE IS EVERYTHING

Page 20

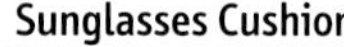

Sunglasses Cushion

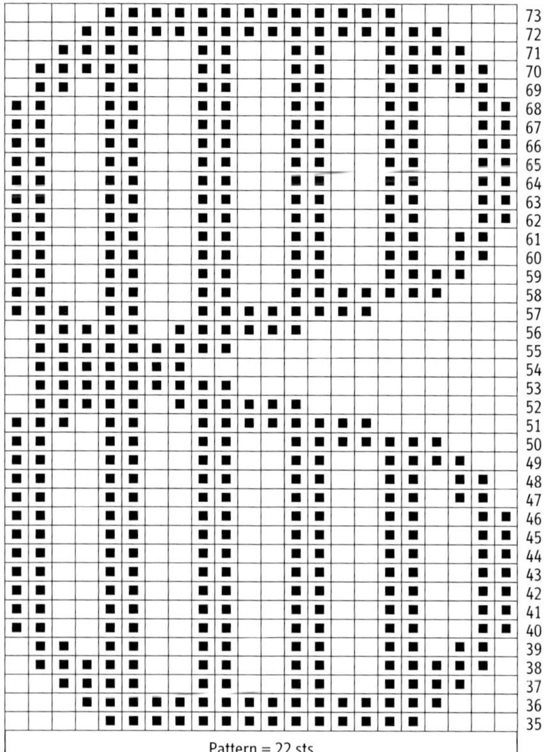

☐ = White

■ = Black

Bowtie Cushion

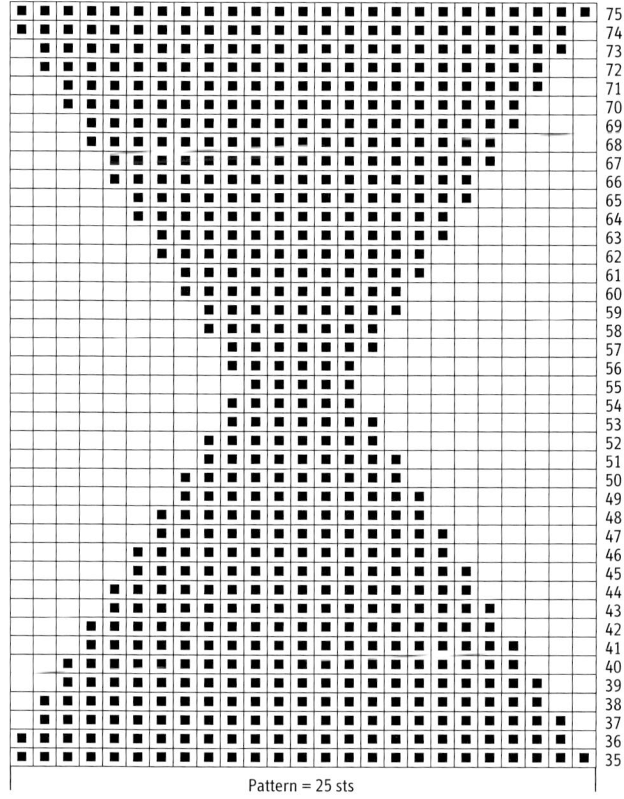

☐ = White

■ = Black

STYLE IS EVERYTHING

Page 20

Mustache Cushion

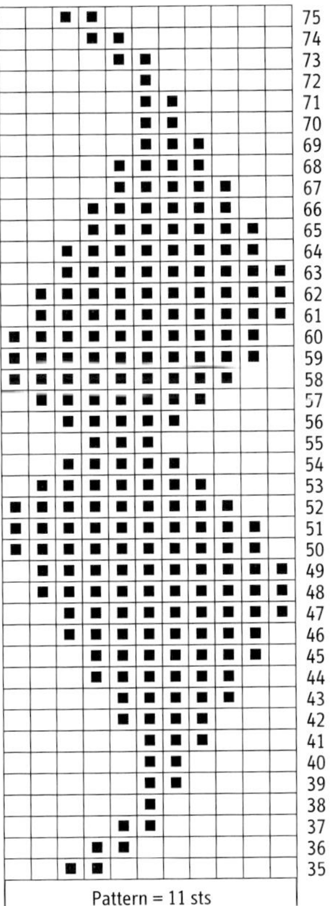

CONCEALED IN BLACK AND WHITE

Page 57

Phone Cover

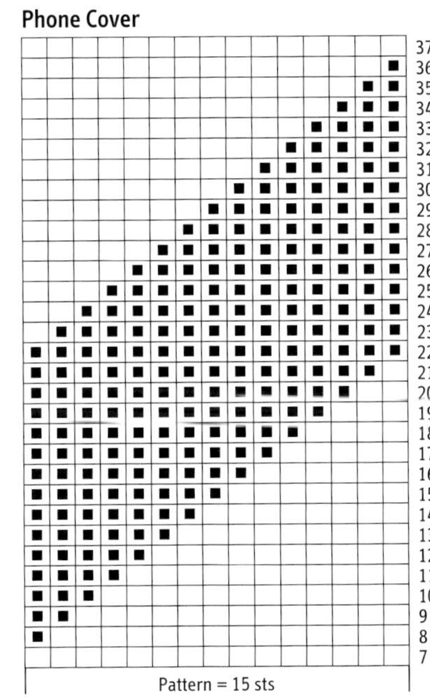

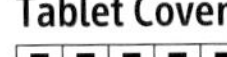

Tablet Cover

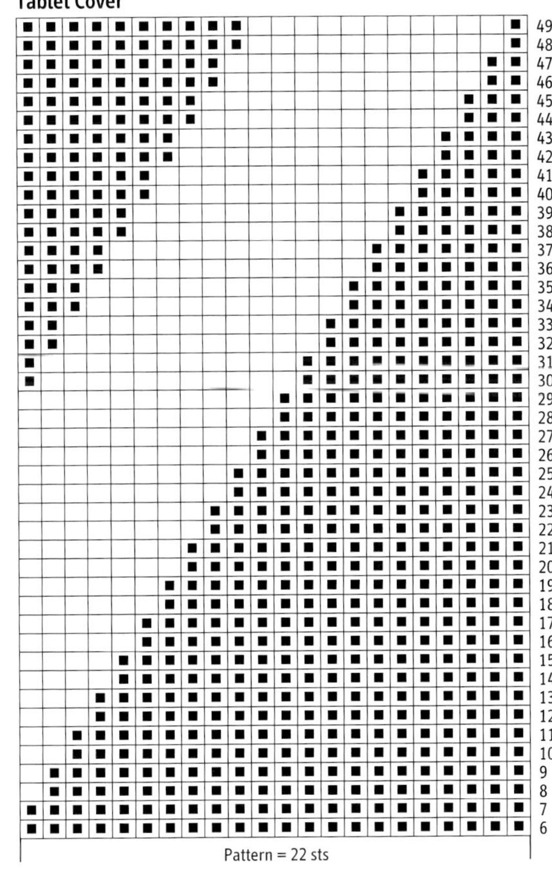

PAINT IT BLACK

Page 37

Play

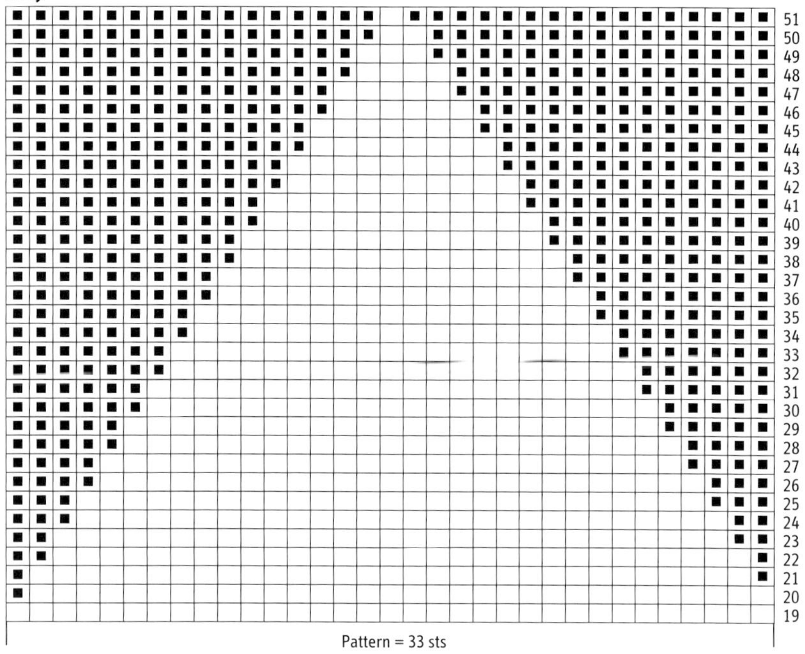

□ = White
■ = Black

PRACTICAL SQUARES

Page 29

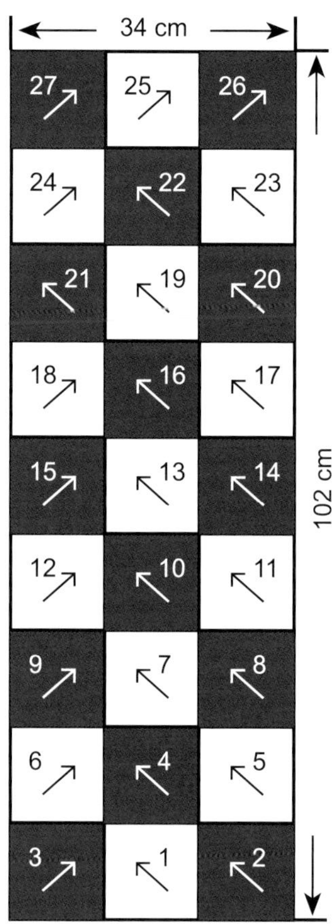

Legend

■ = Black
□ = White
↗ = Direction of diagonal decrease line

HEART OVER HEAD

Page 42

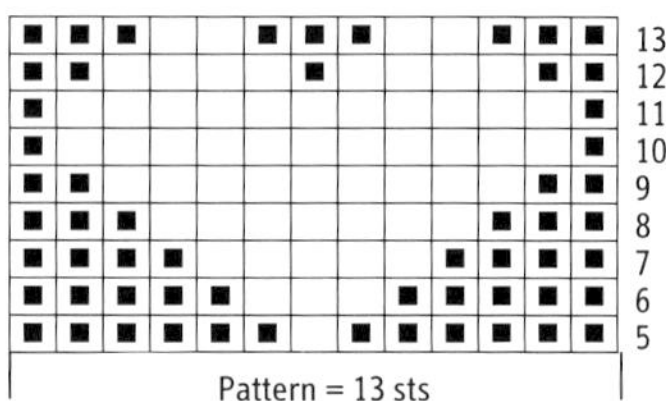

□ = White
■ = Black

CLOSE TO MY HEART

Page 46

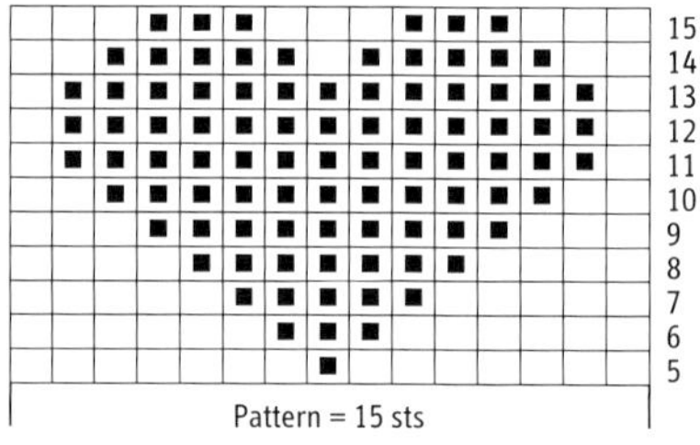

□ = White
■ = Black

COOL STORAGE

Page 70

Small Basket

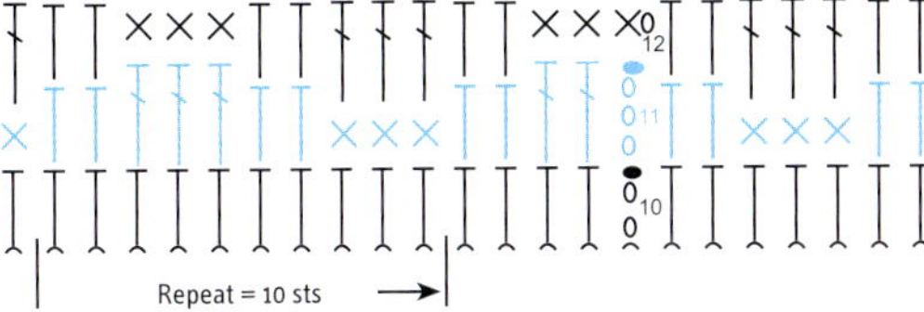

Medium Basket

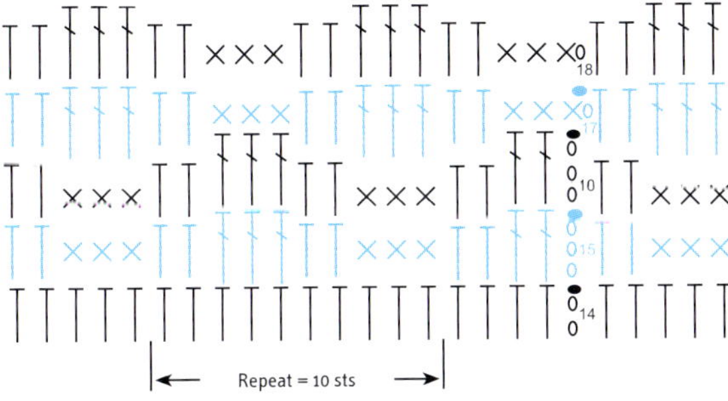

Large Basket

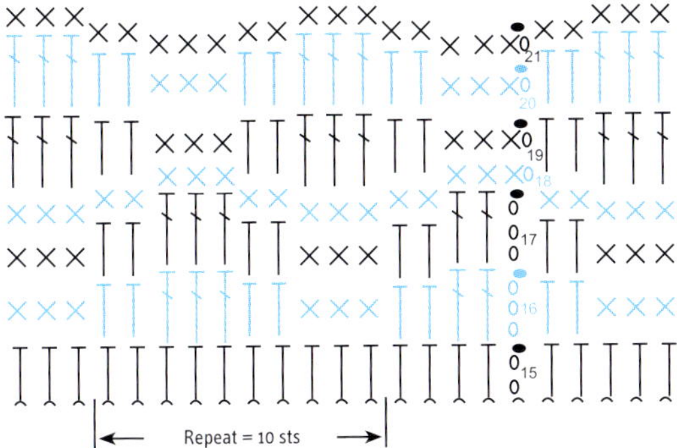

CHART KEY

• = Slip stitch (sl st)

○ = Chain (ch)

× = Single crochet (sc)

= Half double crochet (hdc)

= Back loop half double crochet (bl-hdc)

= Double crochet (dc)

= Treble crochet (tr)

Worked in columns with each stitch being worked into the stitch below.

MAKING WAVES

Page 62

Chart A

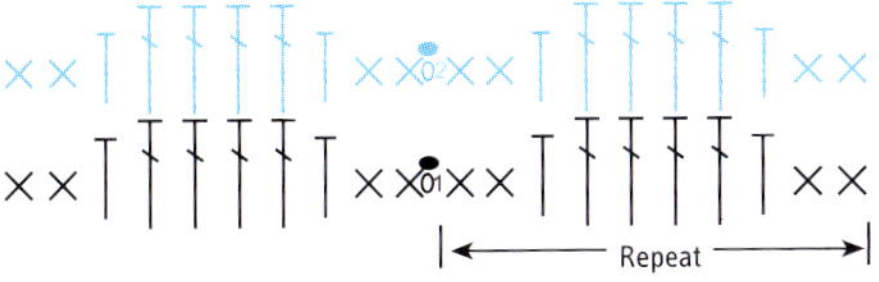

Chart B

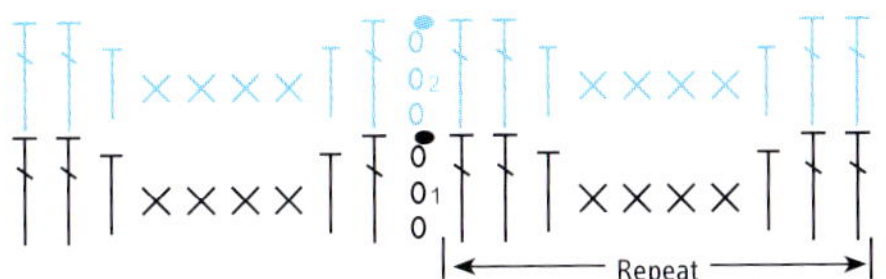

BLACK AND WHITE STORIES

Page 49

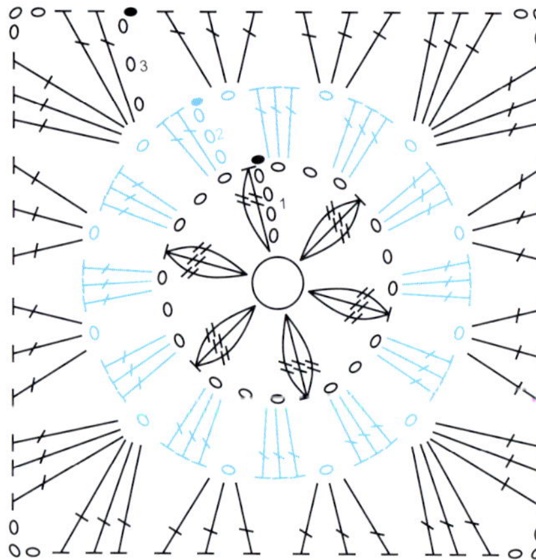

MUSIC IS MY FIRST LOVE

Page 6

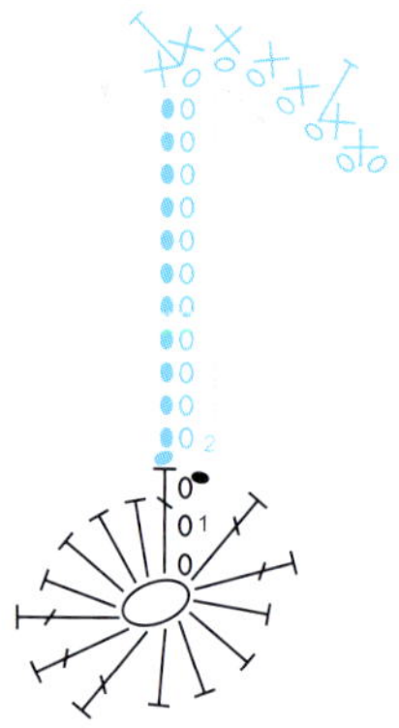

CHART KEY

• = Slip stitch (sl st)

○ = Chain (ch)

× = Single crochet (sc)

= Half double crochet (hdc)

= Back loop half double crochet (bl-hdc)

= Double crochet (dc)

= Treble crochet (tr)

Worked in columns with each stitch being worked into the stitch below.

TABLE LINENS JUST FOR YOU

Page 86

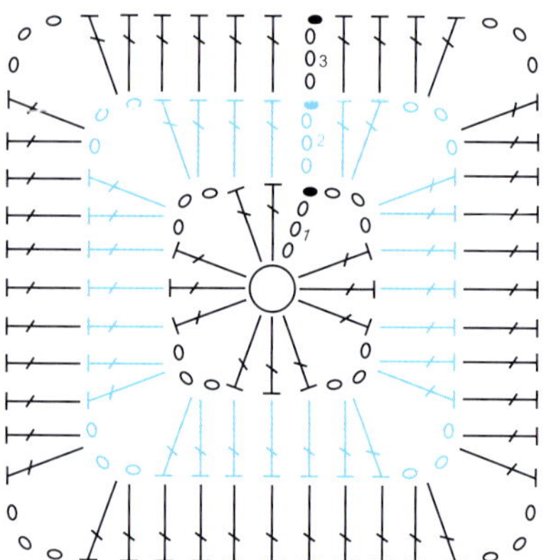

BASIC TECHNIQUES

FOUNDATION CHAIN

Before you begin crocheting, you must make a foundation chain, beginning with a slip knot.

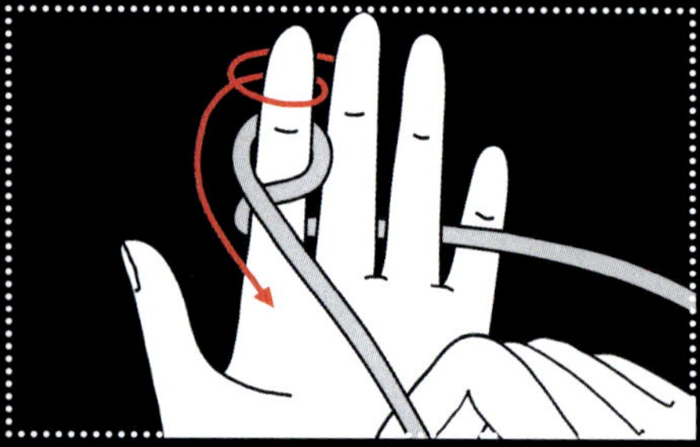

1. Run the tail of the yarn in front of your little finger and behind your ring finger and middle finger for tension, then wrap it around your index finger as shown...

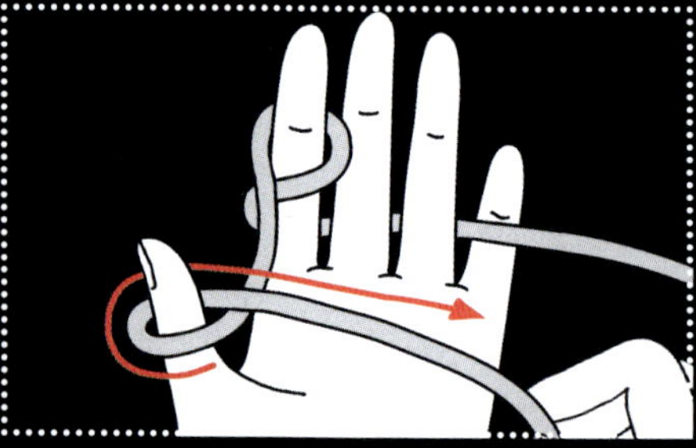

2. ... then wrap the yarn around your thumb with the yarn attached to the ball lying over your palm.

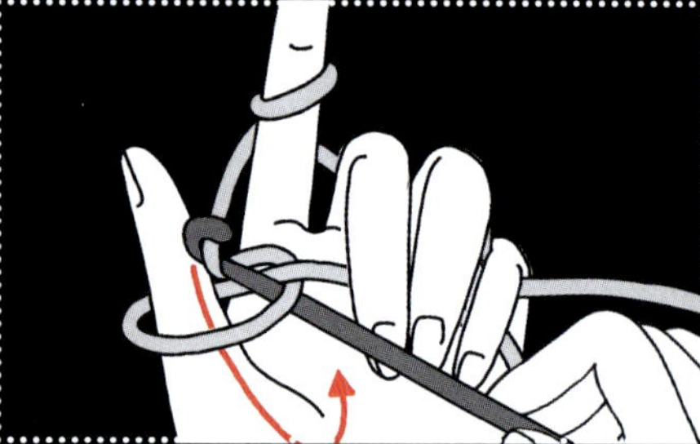

3. Insert the hook into the loop on your thumb and catch the yarn strand that is between your index finger and thumb.

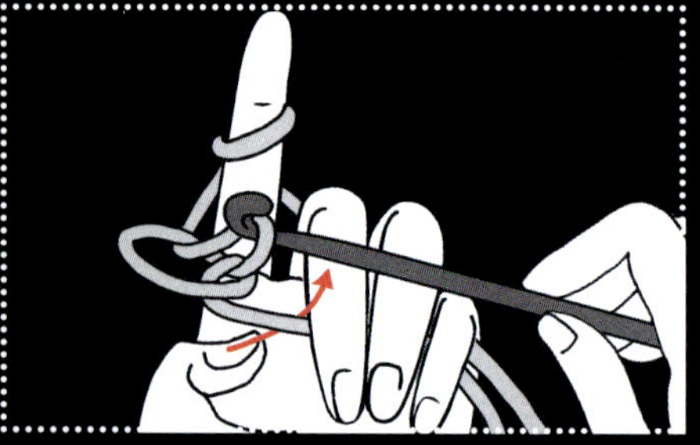

4. Draw the working yarn back through the loop on your thumb, using your middle finger, ring finger, and little finger to hold the yarn tail in place.

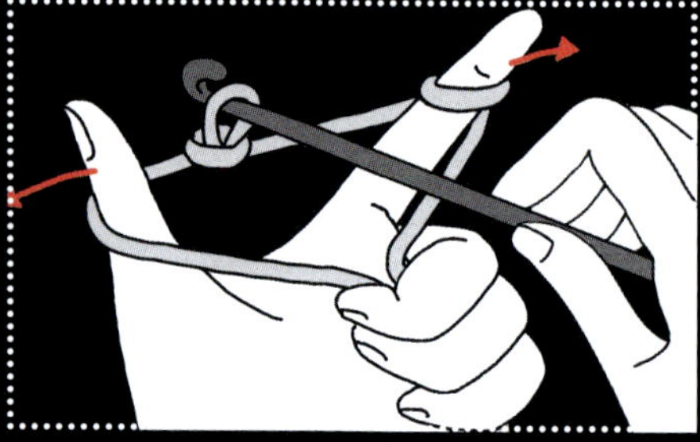

5. Pull your thumb and index finger in place to tighten the first chain. The slip knot is complete.

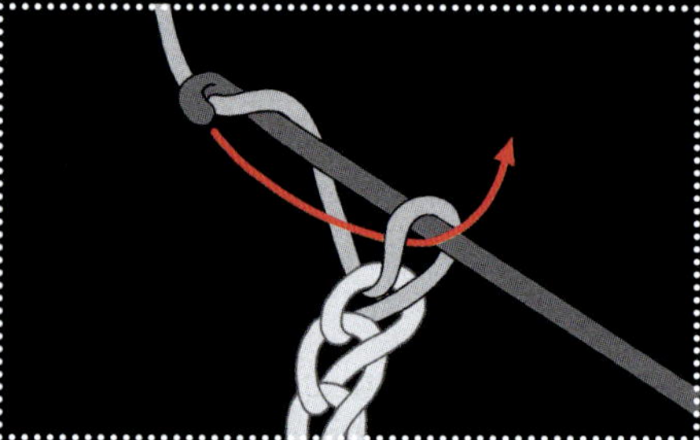

6. To make chain stitches, draw the working yarn through the loop on the hook. Repeat step 6 until you have as many chains as needed.

JOINING A CHAIN TO FORM A RING

First, make a chain with the specified number of stitches. Then, join the chain into a ring by working a slip stitch into the first chain worked as follows: insert the hook into the first chain, draw the yarn through the chain and through the loop on the hook.

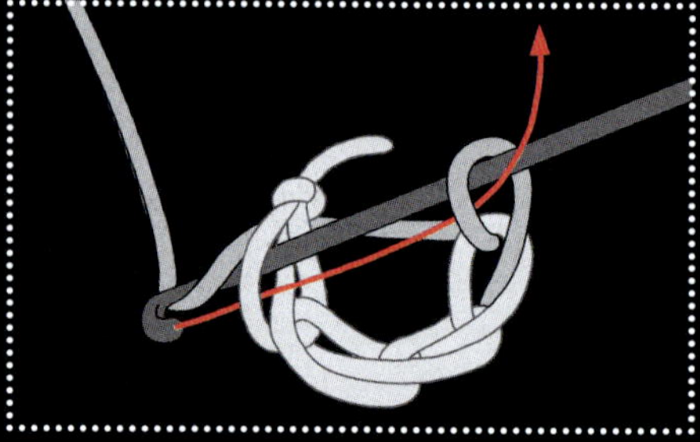

TURNING CHAINS

When working in rows, each row begins with a turning chain to bring the yarn up to the proper height to begin working the next row. The turning chain counts as the first stitch in the row. For single crochet, 1 turning chain is made. For half-double crochet, 2, and for double-crochet 3. If taller stitches are worked, 1 additional turning chain is needed for each extra wrap on the hook (see table).

When working in rounds, the work is not turned but you will still work a chain to bring the yarn up to the proper height to begin the next round. The following chart shows the correct number of chains to work to bring the yarn to the proper height for all basic crochet stitches.

Stitch	Number of Turning Chains
Single crochet	1
Half double crochet	2
Double crochet	3
Treble crochet	4

MAGIC RING

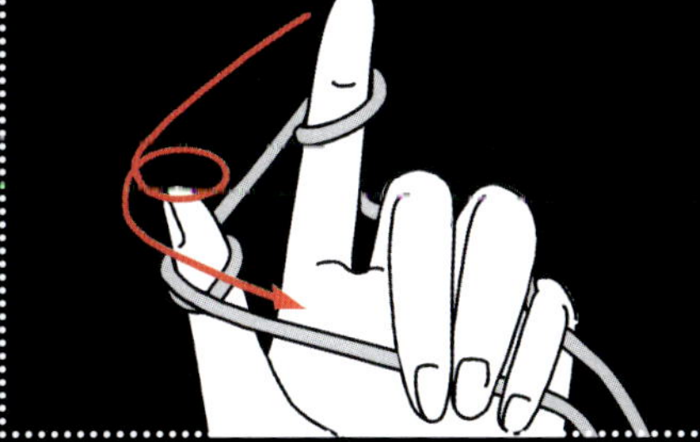

1. Wrap the yarn around your index finger then around your thumb as shown so the yarn is stretched tightly between your finger and thumb.

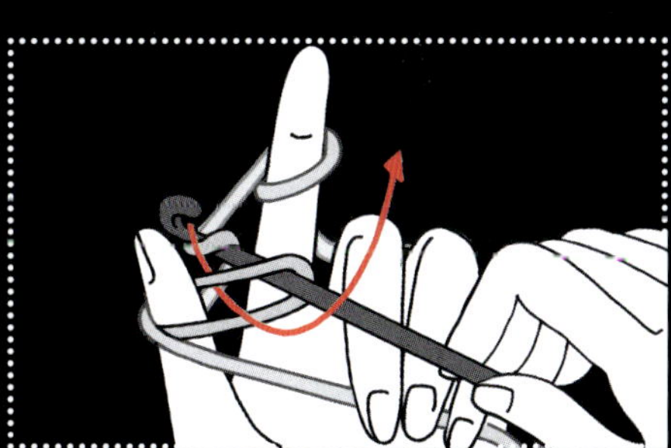

2. Insert the crochet hook into the loop on your thumb and pull the working yarn through.

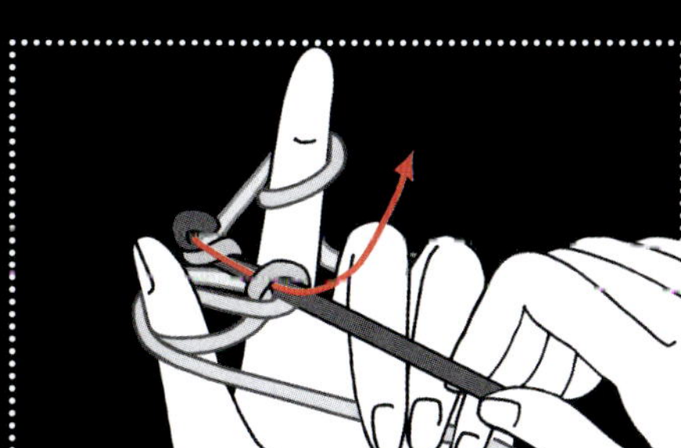

3. Pull the yarn through again to make a chain stitch.

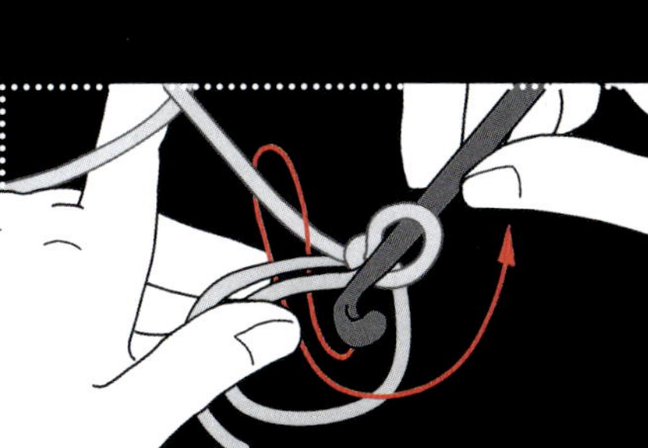

4. To crochet into the ring, insert the hook into the ring and draw up a loop...

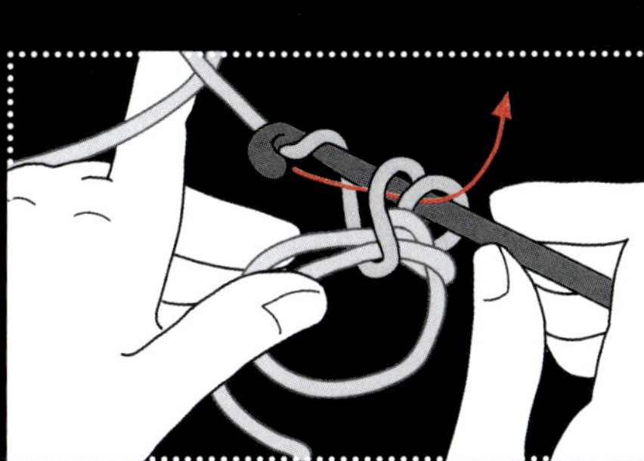

5. Then pull the yarn through both loops on the hook to finish the stitch as a single crochet. Continue crocheting in the ring until you have the desired number of stitches.

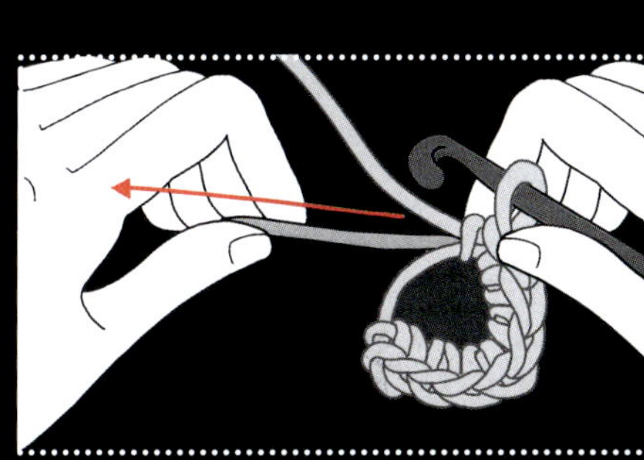

6. When you have made all of the stitches you need, draw the ring closed by gently pulling on the tail, then join the round with a slip stitch.

WORKING SPIRAL ROUNDS

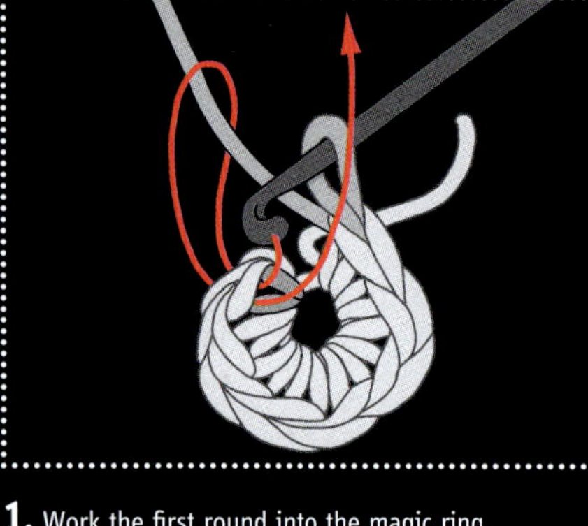

1. Work the first round into the magic ring.

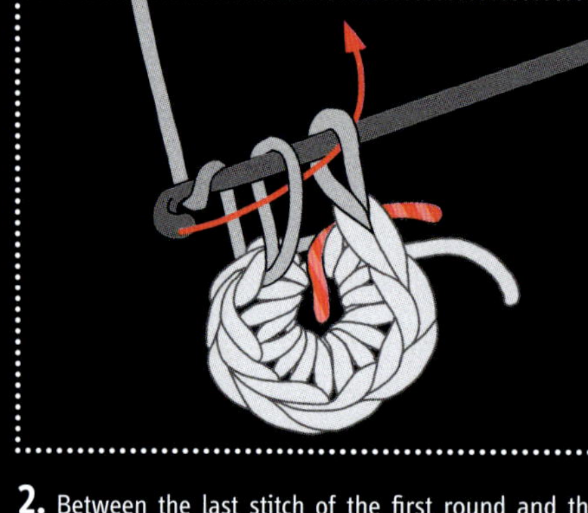

2. Between the last stitch of the first round and the first stitch of the next round, place a piece of contrasting yarn for a marker.

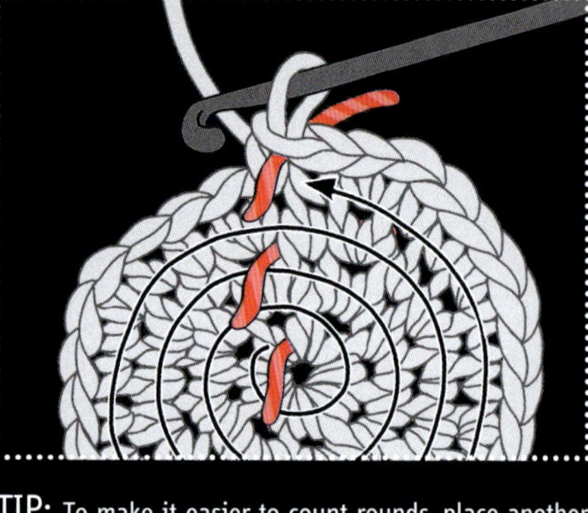

TIP: To make it easier to count rounds, place another thread marker every few rounds.

SINGLE CROCHET

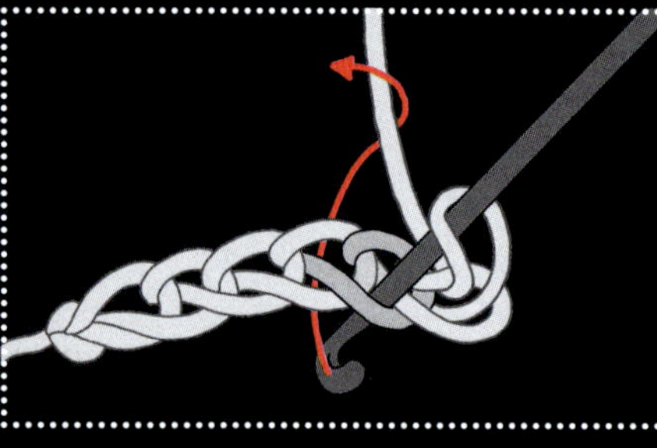

1. Insert the hook into the front of the 2nd chain from the hook and pull up a loop...

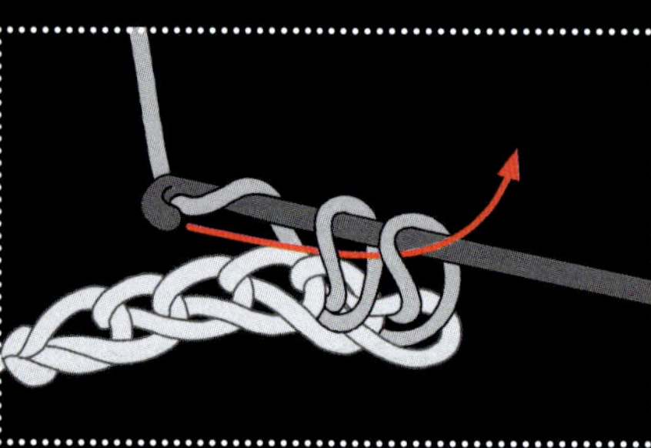

2. Wrap the yarn around the hook and draw the yarn through both loops on the hook.

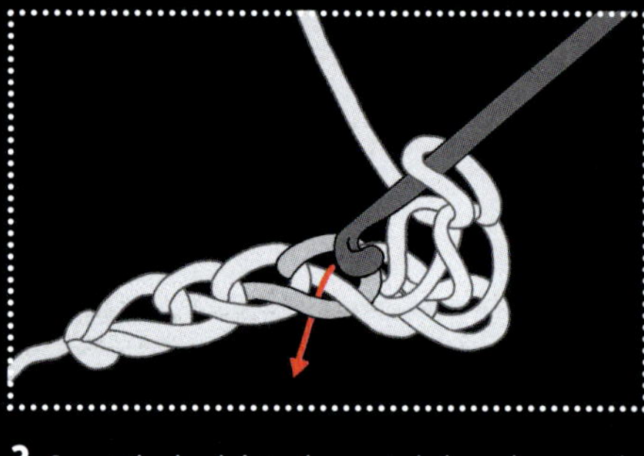

3. Insert the hook into the next chain and repeat the steps.

TIP: When working in rows, the work is turned after each row is complete. The new row is begun by working one chain stitch; then insert the hook into the next stitch on the previous row and begin working single crochet.

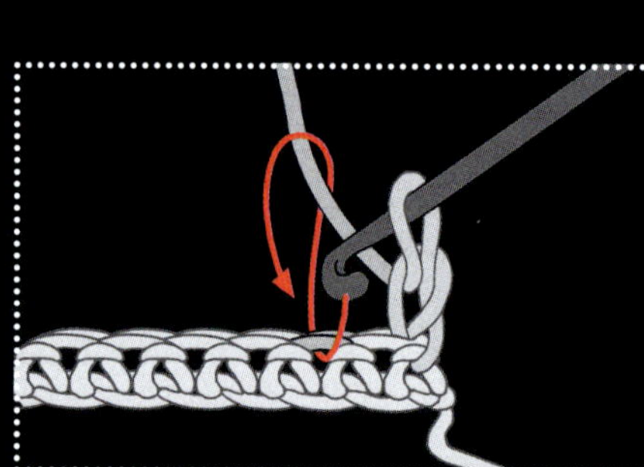

SLIP STITCH

Insert the hook into the next stitch and pull the working yarn through the stitch and through the loop on the hook.

HALF DOUBLE CROCHET

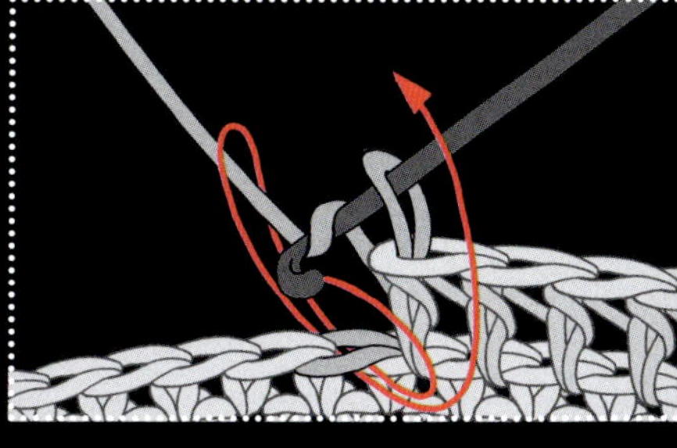

1. Wrap the yarn around the hook then insert the hook into the next stitch and draw up another loop.

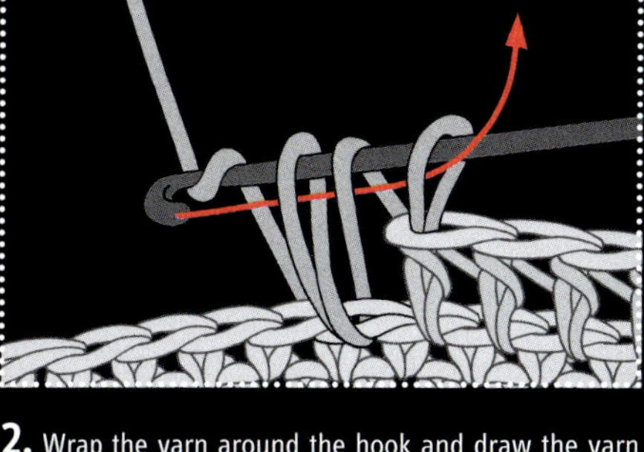

2. Wrap the yarn around the hook and draw the yarn through all 3 loops on the hook.

DOUBLE CROCHET

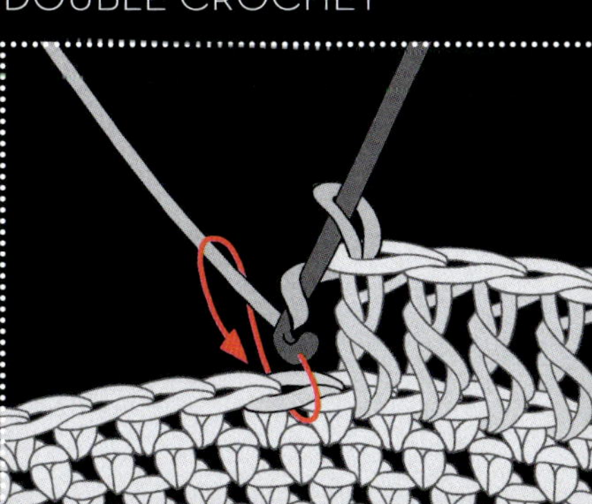

1. Wrap the yarn around the hook then insert the hook into the next stitch and draw up another loop.

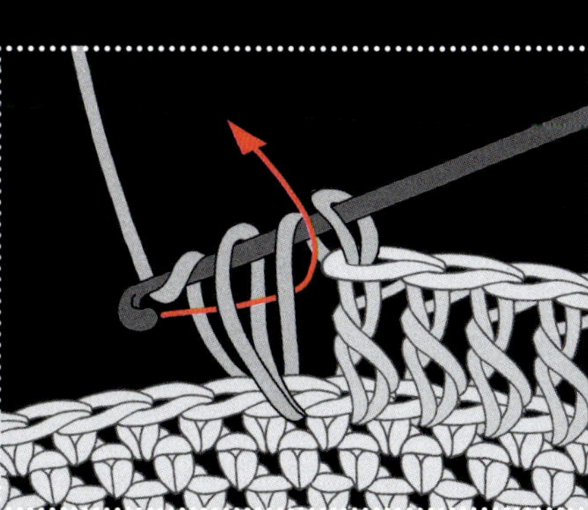

2. Wrap the yarn around the hook and pull the working yarn through 2 loops.

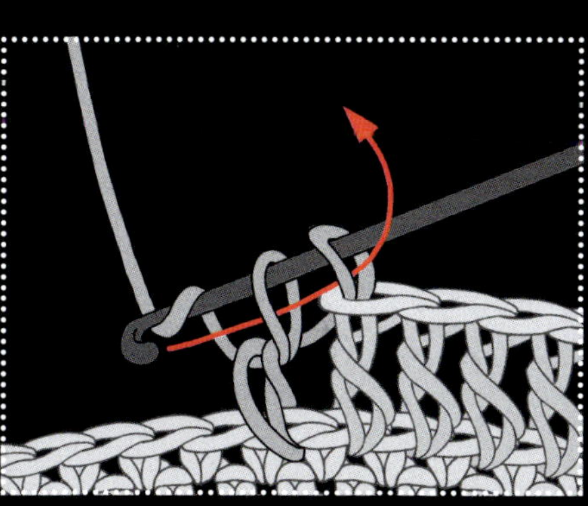

3. Wrap the yarn around the hook and pull the working yarn through the last 2 loops on the hook.

TREBLE CROCHET

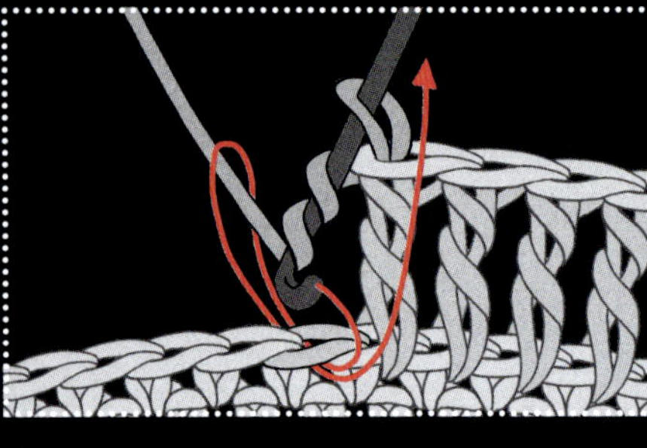

1. Wrap the yarn around the hook twice then insert the hook into the next stitch and draw up another loop.

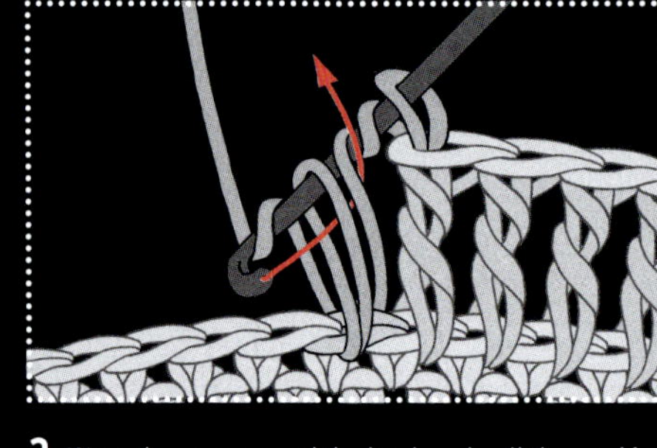

2. Wrap the yarn around the hook and pull the working yarn through 2 loops.

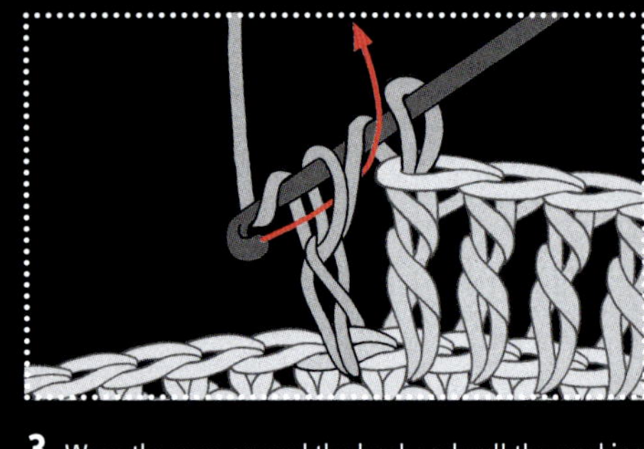

3. Wrap the yarn around the hook and pull the working yarn through 2 loops again.

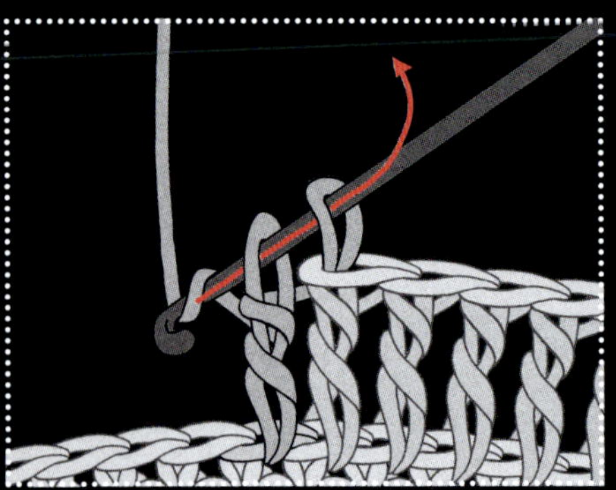

4. Wrap the yarn around the hook and pull the working yarn through the last 2 loops on the hook.

ELONGATED DOUBLE CROCHET

Make 1 normal double crochet then work into the chain space two rows below to make the next double crochet.

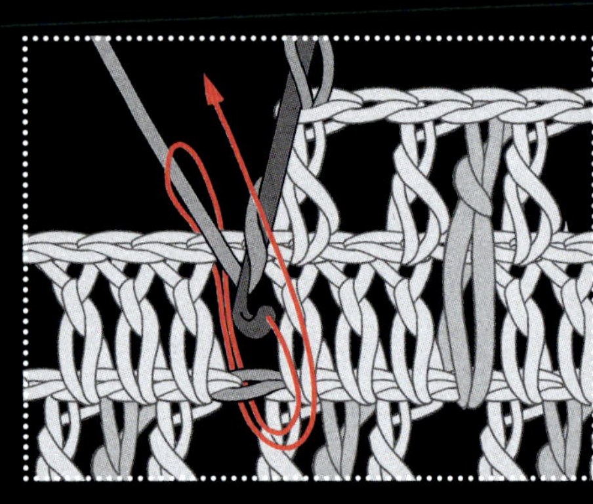

FRONT POST DOUBLE CROCHET

1. Wrap the yarn around the hook then insert the hook around the post of the next double in the previous row from left to right and draw up a loop.

2. Wrap the yarn around the hook and pull the working yarn through 2 loops. Wrap the yarn around the hook again and pull the working yarn through the last 2 loops on the hook.

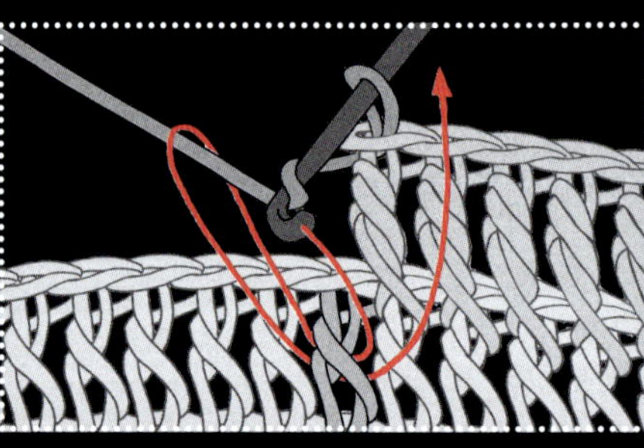

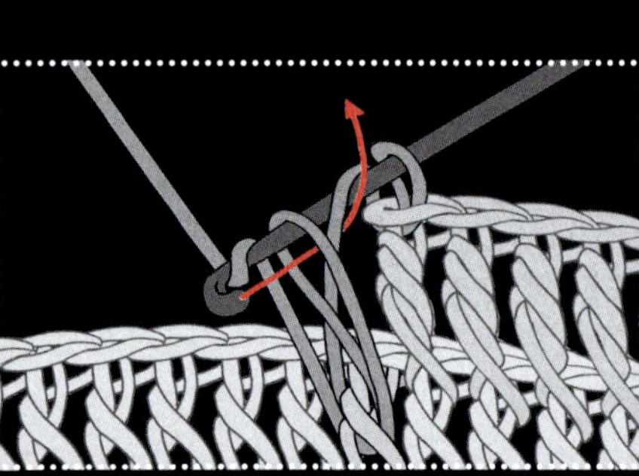

DECREASING

To make a piece narrower, stitches must be decreased.

SINGLE CROCHET DECREASE (SC2TOG)

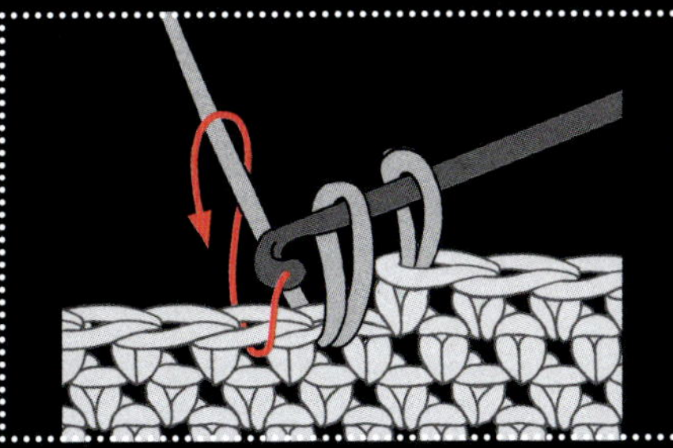

1. Insert the hook into the next stitch and draw up a loop, then insert the hook into the following stitch and draw up another loop.

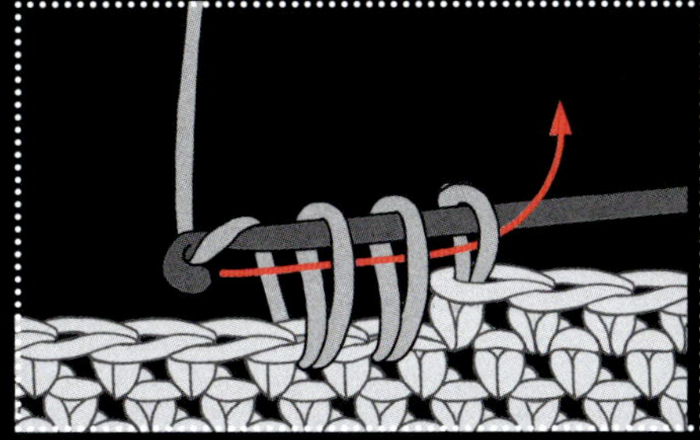

2. Wrap the yarn around the hook and pull the working yarn through all 3 loops on the hook. Two stitches have been decreased to one.

DOUBLE CROCHET DECREASE (DC2TOG)

Wrap yarn around hook, insert hook into next st and draw up a loop (3 loops on hook). Wrap yarn around hook and draw yarn through 2 loops on hook (2 loops remain on hook). Wrap yarn around hook, insert hook into next st and draw up a loop (3 loops on hook). Wrap yarn around hook and draw yarn through all 3 loops on hook.

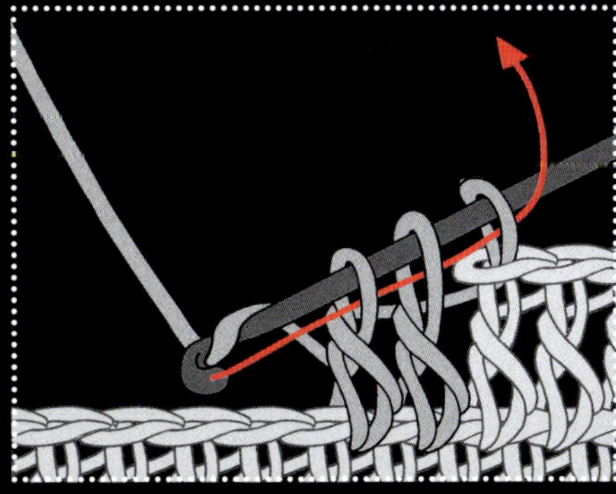

SKIPPING STITCHES TO DECREASE

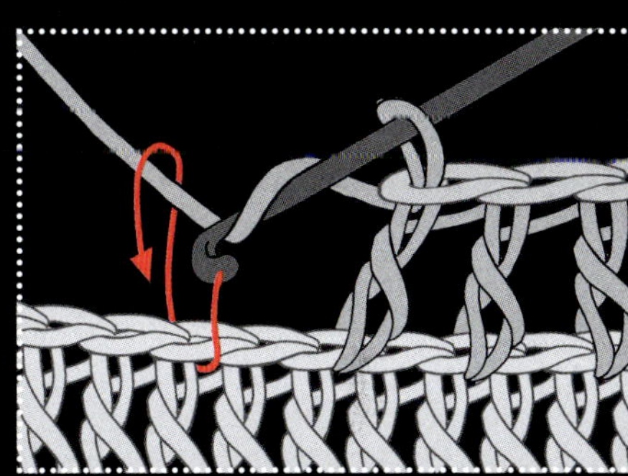

You can also decrease by not working into every stitch. Skip the next st and work into the stitch after.

INCREASING

To increase, work 2 stitches into the same stitch on the previous row. You can increase in this fashion for all types of crochet stitches. This increase can be used when working in rows and when working in the round.

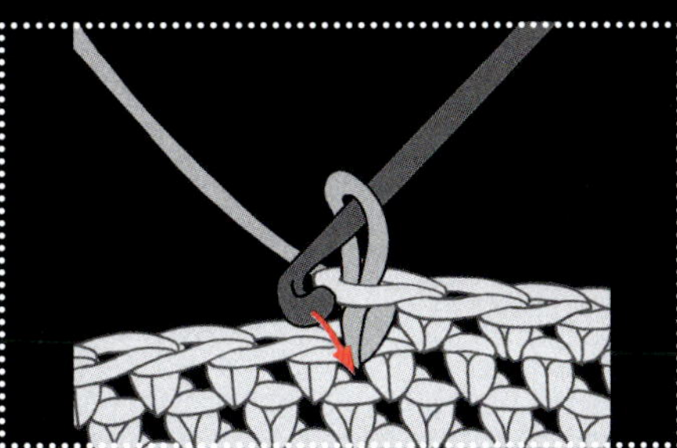

DIRECTION OF CROCHETING

Crab stitch is also called reverse single crochet because it is worked from left to right.

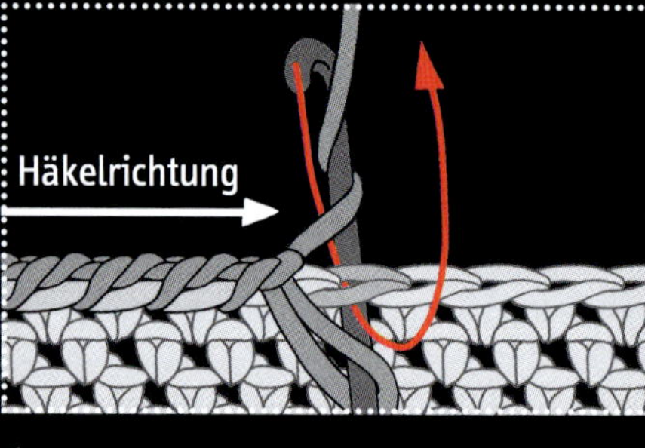

1. Insert the hook into the next stitch to the right of where the yarn is attached. Twist the yarn around the hook and draw through a loop, making sure to bring the new loop up from underneath the old loop.

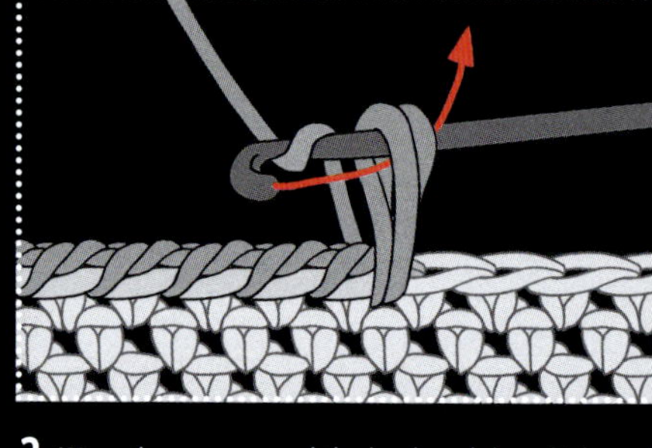

2. Wrap the yarn around the hook and draw it through both loops on the hook.

CHANGING COLORS

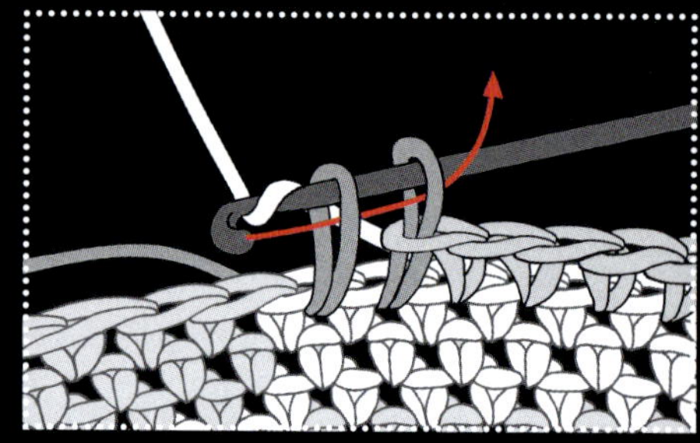

To change colors, work to the last part of the stitch with the old color, leaving 2 loops on the hook. Change to the new color and draw the yarn through to complete the stitch. With this technique, the last loop of the previous stitch is completed with the new color to form a smooth transition.

SEAMS

BACK STITCH

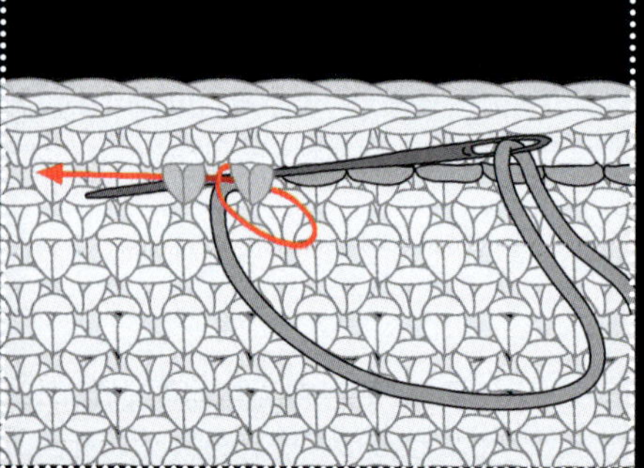

Back stitch is worked firmly just inside the edge of the crochet, with RS together on the pieces being seamed. Use pins to hold the pieces together so they don't move while sewing. Insert the needle from front to back, then from back to front. Repeat this, and to begin each stitch, put the needle into the same space the previous stitch ended.

OVERHAND STITCH

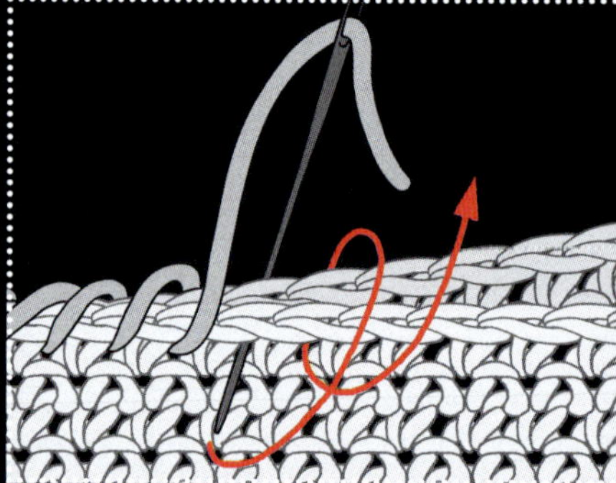

Overhand stitch is worked evenly around the edge of a piece. Put both pieces together with WS facing in. Insert the needle from back to front in the desired spot. Repeat this across the entire seam.

MAKING POMPOMS

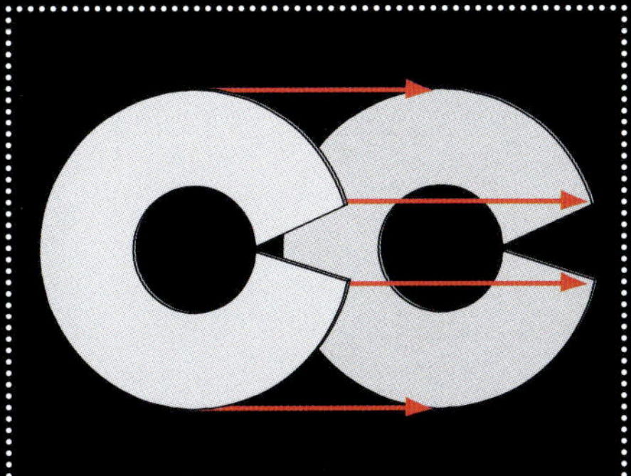

1. Cut two pieces of cardboard into circles the diameter of the desired pompom to create your own pompom maker. Cut a V-shaped slit into both pieces and line them up together.

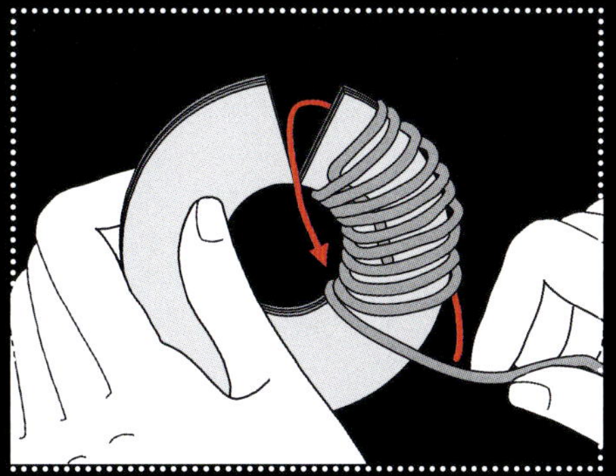

2. Wrap the yarn around and around the two discs until the hole in the middle is completely filled with yarn, using the slit to wrap the yarn.

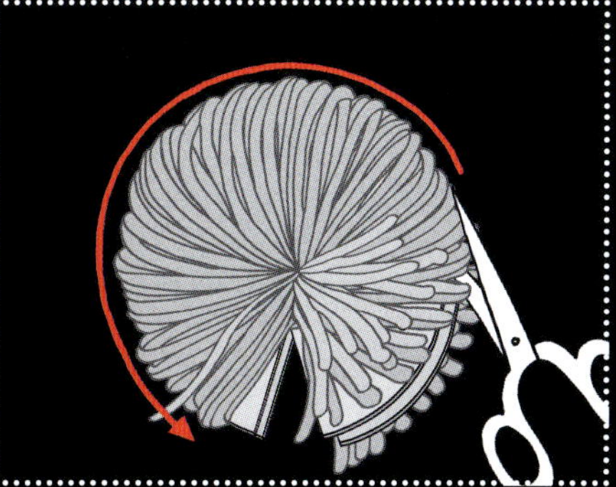

3. Cut the yarn around the outside edge.

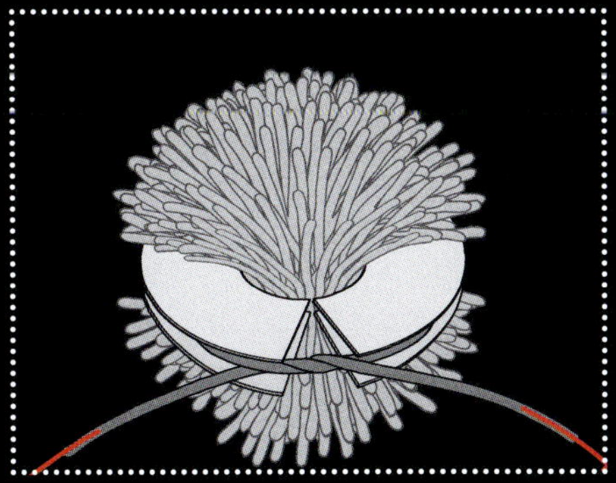

4. Run a strand of yarn around the pompom maker between the two pieces and tie tightly to secure. Then remove the pompom maker.

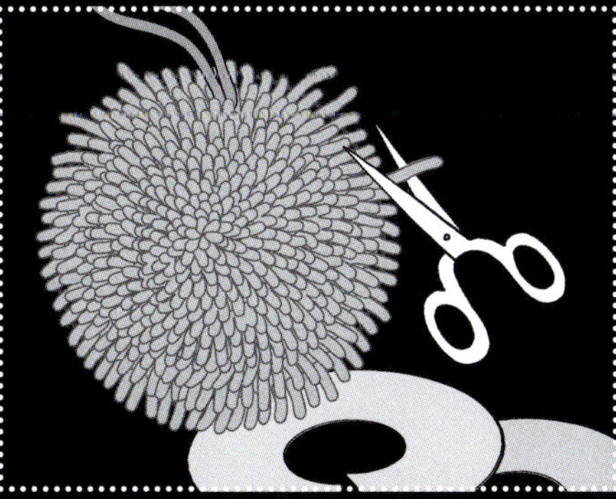

5. Trim the ends of the yarn strands evenly.

ABBREVIATIONS

beg	begin(s)(ning)
ch	chain
cm	centimeter(s)
dc	double crochet (British treble crochet)
fpdc	front post double crochet (British front post treble crochet)
hdc	half double crochet (British half treble crochet)
hk	hook
in	inch(es)
lp(s)	loop(s)
mm	millimeter(s)
rem	remain(s) (ing)
rep	repeat
rnd(s)	round(s)
RS	right side
sc	single crochet (British double crochet)
sk	skip
sl	slip
st(s)	stitch(es)
tog	together
tr	treble (British double treble)
WS	wrong side
yo	yarnover/yarn around hook (British yarn over hook/yoh)

YARN INFORMATION

Webs – America's Yarn Store
75 Service Center Road
Northampton, MA 01060
800-367-9327
www.yarn.com
customerservice@yarn.com

Westminster Fibers (in US)
8 Shelter Drive
Greer, SC 29650
800-445-9276
www.westminsterfibers.com
info@westminsterfibers.com

(in Canada)
10 Roybridge Gate, Suite 200
Vaughan, ON L4H 3M8
800-263-2354

If you are unable to obtain any of the yarn used in this book, it can be replaced with a yarn of a similar weight and composition. Please note, however, the finished projects may vary slightly from those shown, depending on the yarn used. Try www.yarnsub.com for suggestions.

For more information on selecting or substituting yarn, contact your local yarn shop or an online store; they are familiar with all types of yarns and would be happy to help you. Additionally, the online knitting community at Ravelry.com has forums where you can post questions about specific yarns. Yarns come and go so quickly these days and there are so many beautiful yarns available.

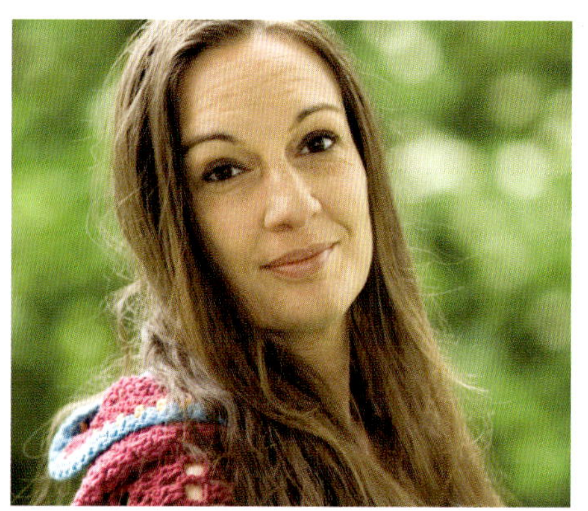

CONSTANZE DIEHL-HUPFER has been working with fiber since she was a child. She has spent many hours working with wool, weaving, and crochet. During her career in the medical field, she lacked the opportunity to develop creatively so she began painting with acrylics in her free time. After her children were born, she began sewing children's clothes and accessories. In 2011, she began selling her handmade garments under the label D.SIGN. In 2013, she opened an internet shop where she sells her handmade pieces as well as yarn and supplies.

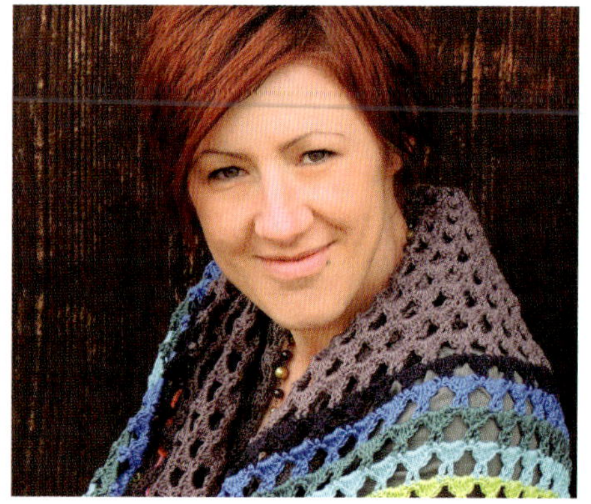

MAGDALENA MELZER is 36 years old and lives with her husband and their four children in Memmingen-Allgäu in the Swabia region of Germany. She discovered her love for handcrafts as a child and it became her profession, where she could develop her creativity. In 2012 she opened her own company, "Curlyz", to pursue her passions for designing and crocheting colorful creations.

Thank you! Special thanks to my wonderful family, to my children for their unending patience, to my husband for always having my back and believing in me! And special thanks to my friend Conni for her wonderful support and collaboration!